GEORGE W. NORRIS ☆ *Gentle Knight of American Democracy*

☆ ☆ ☆ ☆ ☆ ☆ ☆ ☆ ☆

GEORGE W. NORRIS

Gentle Knight of American Democracy

☆ ☆ ☆ ☆ ☆ ☆ ☆ ☆ ☆

by Norman L. Zucker

UNIVERSITY OF ILLINOIS PRESS, URBANA AND LONDON, 1966

☆ ☆ ☆ ☆ ☆ ☆ ☆ ☆ ☆

WINGATE COLLEGE LIBRARY
WINGATE, N C

A section of Chapter Four and Chapter Five have appeared in somewhat different form in *Nebraska History*. Portions of Chapter Six have appeared in *The Progressive*.

☆　　☆　　☆　　☆　　☆　　☆　　☆　　☆　　☆

© 1966 by the Board of Trustees of the University of Illinois. Manufactured in the United States of America. Library of Congress Catalog Card No. 66-10060.

TO MY MOTHER AND THE MEMORY OF MY FATHER

33555

Preface

☆　　☆　　☆　　☆　　☆　　☆　　☆　　☆　　☆

It is an unpleasant commentary on American politics in the second half of the twentieth century that morality in politics elicits sustained praise as being most commendable and difficult of achievement rather than being casually accepted as a standard norm of behavior. This truism, in turn, is related to the larger and even more unpleasant contemporary syndrome which considers idealism in domestic politics either a mischievous and passing aberration, or a pragmatic expression securely related to the next election. But this was not always the prevailing ethos. American politics at the beginning of the twentieth century were permeated with a vigorous and dynamic moral idealism which, when translated into political action, became the progressive movement.

This movement or, more accurately, these movements (recent scholarship has produced a wealth of rich — and sometimes conflicting — interpretations of the causal forces that shaped and directed them) gave rise to a host of men who left their image on the American scene. Among them was George W. Norris. He was a throwback to populism, a link between the progressive period and the New Deal, and a bridge between the throbbing reform waves of the farm and the city. From his long and fruitful career,

Norris of Nebraska emerged, not only with a significant legislative history, but also as a symbol of rectitude, integrity, and decency in the American political process.

Impressed by both Norris' considerable legislative achievements and his unswerving political virtue, I have tried to outline selectively the political record and philosophy of Senator Norris and relate them to the twentieth-century American political reform tradition.

Boston, Massachusetts   NORMAN L. ZUCKER

Acknowledgments

☆　　☆　　☆　　☆　　☆　　☆　　☆　　☆　　☆

One of the more pleasant tasks associated with writing a book is to acknowledge the assistance so necessary for its completion. The basic research was done at Rutgers University, as was the writing of the first draft of the manuscript. I am, accordingly, indebted to the staff of the Rutgers University Library, particularly Gilbert Kelley and Rose Sieber Czapp of the Reference Division, Joan Cassera, Eugene Doleschal, and François-X. Grondin of the Government Documents Division, who gave assistance far beyond the normally extended limits set by librarians. The personnel of the Manuscripts Division of the Library of Congress, especially Fred Klein, were exceedingly helpful during my examination of the Norris Papers. The final draft was completed at Tufts University, where I constantly availed myself of the courteous services extended by the staff of the Eaton Library.

Rutgers Professors Benjamin Baker, Ardath W. Burks, Richard P. McCormick, Eugene Meehan, and the late Norman L. Stamps always gave generously of their time, good counsel, and friendship. Professor Richard Lowitt of Connecticut College, laboring in the same vineyard, unhesitatingly supplied some of his own unpublished material. At Tufts, Professor James V. Elliot made valuable criticisms of the manuscript and Professor Robert R. Robbins shielded me from an excess of arid committee assignments and fostered a gracious and congenial departmental atmosphere. The Tufts University Faculty Research Fund provided the wherewithal for the very excellent services of Mrs. Stella Briere, who with diligence and perception not only transcribed my crabbed writing into typescript, but also caught errors and corrected faulty spelling.

This study, however, could not have reached fruition without the help of two people: Edward McNall Burns, emeritus professor and chairman of the Rutgers Department of Political Science, who read the entire manuscript, suggested sundry improvements, and provided nourishing guidance and inspiration; and my wife, Naomi, who proofread, edited, and, most importantly, with gentle humor pampered me through author's dyspepsia and doldrums.

Contents

☆   ☆   ☆   ☆   ☆   ☆   ☆   ☆

☆　☆　☆　☆　☆　☆　☆　☆　☆

"History asks 'Did the man have integrity? Did the man have unselfishness? Did the man have courage? Did the man have consistency?'

"And if the individual under the scrutiny of the historic microscope measured up to an affirmative answer to these questions, then history has set him down as great indeed in the pages of all the years to come.

"There are few statesmen in America today who so definitely and clearly measure up to an affirmative answer to the four questions as does the senior Senator from Nebraska, George W. Norris. In his rare case, history has already written the verdict. . . .

"He stands forth as the very perfect, gentle knight of American progressive ideals."

☆　☆　☆　☆　☆　☆　☆　☆　☆

FRANKLIN D. ROOSEVELT
McCook, Nebraska
September 29, 1932

☆ ☆ ☆ ☆ ☆ ☆ ☆ ☆ ☆

CHAPTER ONE

The Genesis of a Democrat

☆ ☆ ☆ ☆ ☆ ☆ ☆ ☆ ☆

George William Norris of Nebraska is a folk hero of American political history. The phrase "Norris of Nebraska" has come to be synonymous with the characteristics of independence, integrity, and liberalism. Serving continuously in Congress from the Republican Roosevelt's Square Deal to the Democratic Roosevelt's New Deal, he was retired from the Senate as the acknowledged Grand Old Man of Progressivism. Such lengthy service is indeed a remarkable feat; but political longevity in itself only assumes significance when considered in relation to the party system and a record of achievement. In both these areas Norris was unique.

George W. Norris began his legislative career in 1903, as a Republican in the House of Representatives, and concluded it in 1942, when, as an Independent, he was defeated for reelection to the Senate. Although nominally a Republican until his Independent candidacy in 1936, he defied powerful Republican Speaker Joseph G. Cannon on the issue of party regularity; engaged in an insurgent controversy with President William Howard Taft; fought alongside Bull Mooser Theodore Roosevelt in his 1912 battle at Armageddon; supported President Woodrow Wilson's New Freedom reforms; constantly and bitterly opposed the business philosophy of the Republican administrations of Harding, Coolidge, and Hoover; and ultimately emerged as an outspoken advocate of President Franklin D. Roosevelt's New Deal.

More important than his political aberrations, however, was the Nebraskan's highly significant legislative legacy which is part of the twentieth-century progressive reform impulse of American politics. Senator Norris substantially reformed the rules of the House of Representatives, sponsored major legislation of lasting importance for agriculture and labor, fathered visionary bills which created the Tennessee Valley Authority and the Twentieth Amendment to the Constitution, and was primarily responsible for the successful establishment in Nebraska of the only unicameral legislature in the United States.

THE FRONTIER YEARS

George William Norris, like so many other Americans, rose to prominence from humble beginnings. He was born shortly after the start of the Civil War, on July 11, 1861, to Chauncey and Mary Mook Norris,[1] in York Township, Ohio, a typical midwestern town rapidly emerging from its pioneer beginnings.[2] The young Norris worked his way through Northern Indiana Normal School, now Valparaiso University, where he earned both a Bachelor's and a law degree. His formal education completed at the age of twenty-two, he returned, in 1883, to his mother's farm and became first a clerk in a local law office and then a teacher in the district school.[3] But Norris hoped for better opportunities and sought them by going west to the Pacific Northwest. The Washington Territory,

[1] Biographical data on Norris may be found in a number of articles and in the following books: Richard L. Neuberger and Stephen B. Kahn, *Integrity: The Life of George W. Norris* (New York: Vanguard Press, 1937). Alfred Lief, *Democracy's Norris: The Biography of a Lonely Crusade* (New York: Stackpole Sons, 1939). George W. Norris, *Fighting Liberal: The Autobiography of George W. Norris* (New York: The Macmillan Company, 1945). Richard Lowitt, *George W. Norris: The Making of a Progressive, 1861–1912* (Syracuse: Syracuse University Press, 1963). Norris' Autobiography provides some interesting insights into his character and philosophy. Lowitt's excellent study, not yet published in full, promises to be the definitive biography.
[2] Richard Lowitt, "The Ohio Boyhood of George W. Norris," *Northwest Ohio Quarterly*, XXX (Spring 1958), 70–77.
[3] Richard Lowitt and Randolph C. Downes, eds., "George W. Norris: Monclova Township Schoolmaster," *Northwest Ohio Quarterly*, XXX (Spring 1958), 78–91.

however, was not the promised land which he had anticipated, and, after a period of teaching there, he returned home. His stay in Ohio was brief; in 1885 he established a law practice in Nebraska, an area then enjoying a period of growth and prosperity.[4]

In 1890, when conditions were hard and the Populist party was in its formative stages in the Midwest, Norris made his first bid for political office as prosecuting attorney of Furnas County. "In Kansas and North Dakota," notes Paul W. Glad, "there was one mortgage for every two people, and in Nebraska, South Dakota, and Minnesota there was one for every three."[5] Angry, dispossessed farmers, as in the earlier Greenback and Granger years, again lashed out against the railroads, monopolies, and tight credit. In neighboring Kansas, perhaps the hardest hit financially of all the midwestern states, Mary Ellen Lease, "the Kansas Pythoness," venemously convinced the disgruntled prairie farmers to "raise less corn and more hell." In the Nebraska election of 1890, both houses of the legislature were captured by the Populists. Republican Norris, unable to surmount the wave of angry Populism, had launched his political career disastrously by losing to John T. McClure, a former Democrat who ran as a Populist. Two years later, however, Norris was elected prosecutor and compiled an excellent record as a stern but fair county attorney.

When Norris began a campaign for the district judgeship in 1895, the Populists were still the strongest political group in the area. Nonetheless, Norris defeated the Populist incumbent by two votes and began his judicial career in January 1896. Three years later he was elected to his second and final judicial term.[6] The years in which Norris served as a judge were years of crop failure and low farm prices. Nature and the market had conspired to oppress the farmer. Judge Norris applied common sense as well as judicial precedent in dispensing justice in accordance with the needs of a sod-house society. The principles of Blackstone and Coke were modified to suit the exigencies of the Nebraska prairies. Norris' second term on the bench followed the pattern set by the first, and his reputation and stature grew. In 1902 he secured the Republican

[4] Richard Lowitt, "Norris and Nebraska, 1885–1890," *Nebraska History,* XXXIX (March 1958), 23–39.
[5] Paul W. Glad, *The Trumpet Soundeth: William Jennings Bryan and His Democracy, 1896–1912* (Lincoln: University of Nebraska Press, 1960), p. 48.
[6] Richard Lowitt, "Populism and Politics: The Start of George W. Norris' Political Career," *Nebraska History,* XLII (June 1961), 75–94.

nomination for the Fifth Congressional District and ran against incumbent Ashton C. Shallenberger, who had the support of both Democrats and Populists. Norris edged out his opponent by 181 votes, but was a minority winner because of the few hundred votes cast for the Prohibitionist candidate. The *Oxford Standard* indicated that the chief reason for Norris' success was that "Old General Prosperity and a big crop have this year emblazoned a way to Republican success." [7]

Norris had reclaimed the Fifth Congressional District of eighteen counties in southwestern Nebraska from Populist-Democratic control. He set off for Washington with a weeping-willow mustache, a heavy gold cable watch chain, and an implicit faith in the virtue and wisdom of the Republican party.

PROGRESSIVE IN THE MAKING

When George W. Norris arrived in Washington to take his seat in the Fifty-eighth Congress of 1903, Theodore Roosevelt, successor to the assassinated William McKinley, was in the White House and the progressives and the muckrakers were prodding the national conscience. Muckraking, the journalism of exposure, ran almost parallel to Roosevelt's administration. The movement began in 1902, reached militancy in 1903–4, by 1911 was ebbing, and ultimately, in 1912, merged into progressivism. Called "the publicity men for reform," the muckrakers aroused the public ire and provided the progressives with evidence to support their fight for remedial social and economic legislation. Lincoln Steffens attacked municipal corruption; Ida Tarbell's scholarly exposure of Standard Oil, along with such sensational series as Thomas Lawson's "Frenzied Finance" and David Graham Phillipps' "The Treason of the Senate," aroused national interest. Reformers such as Ray Stannard Baker, Hamlin Garland, Eugene Debs, and George Herron filled the dime magazines with discussions of trust problems, railroad and other monopolies, municipal ownership, and cooperative schemes. The ideology of laissez-faire and Social Darwinism was beginning to crumble as the nation became economically integrated and as the exploding industrial cities began to compete with

[7] Neuberger and Kahn, *op. cit.*, p. 29. Claudius O. Johnson, "George William Norris," *The American Politician*, ed. J. T. Salter (Chapel Hill: University of North Carolina Press, 1938), p. 79.

the countryside for the nation's population. The progressive impulse tried to humanize the existing industrial order, but it did not confine itself to politics, spreading also to economics, history, law, religion, philosophy, and the arts.[8] But Norris, as a neophyte congressman, did not demonstrate any marked liberal tendencies, nor did he even, in the first few years, particularly distinguish himself as a representative. Norris was a very minor congressman, a devoted follower and admirer of Theodore Roosevelt and Speaker Cannon. But with legislative experience came recognition as an able and rising member of the House. In most instances Norris hewed to the Republican party line. His partisanship, however, was not extreme; occasionally he spoke and voted against party measures. These minor deviations, however, did not noticeably damage his standing with Speaker Cannon or the party hierarchy.

As Norris grew more familiar with the legislative process, he developed a strong distaste for the pattern of party regularity which enabled the conservative Eastern wing of the Republican party to dominate policy. He slowly became identified with the insurgents, that group of dissentient congressmen who represented the progressive wing of the Republican party.[9]

The first tangible evidence of insurrection on the part of Norris occurred on May 16, 1908, when he introduced a resolution which provided that all standing committees be appointed by the Committee on Rules. This resolution was sent to the Rules Committee where its chairman, Speaker Cannon, effectively disposed of this threat to his power. This resolution represented Norris' first actual break with the party machine. No longer could he expect the usual "favors and courtesies" that were extended to party stalwarts.[10] He had committed himself to the road of political independence, although he was to retain the Republican party label until his Independent candidacy for the Senate in 1936.

As the administration of President Theodore Roosevelt came to

[8] Arthur and Lila Weinberg, eds., *The Muckrakers, the Era in Journalism That Moved America to Reform — The Most Significant Magazine Articles of 1902–1912* (New York: Simon and Schuster, Inc., 1961), pp. xvi–xviii. Russel B. Nye, *Midwestern Progressive Politics: A Historical Study of Its Origins and Development, 1870–1958* (East Lansing: Michigan State University Press, 1959), *passim.*
[9] Lowitt, *Making of a Progressive, op. cit., passim.*
[10] Kenneth W. Hechler, *Insurgency: Personalities and Politics of the Taft Era* (New York: Columbia University Press, 1940), p. 12.

an end, the insurgents began to gain strength and national recognition. "Czar" Cannon, "The Iron Duke," was seen by the public as an ogre who tyrannized over the House of Representatives and who thwarted the public will. By the end of 1908 reformers were committed to eradicating the evil of Cannonism. Norris succeeded in marshaling this anti-Cannon feeling during the course of the Ballinger-Pinchot controversy over one of America's most notable public land frauds.

In August of 1909, an obscure General Land Office agent, Louis R. Glavis, formally accused President Taft's Secretary of the Interior, Richard A. Ballinger, of conduct indicating his unfitness for high public office. But Ballinger was twice exculpated, first by Attorney General Wickersham and then by President Taft. The Wickersham and Taft exonerations of Ballinger, however, only incited the progressives to greater efforts. After Taft discharged the ardent conservationist Gifford Pinchot, chief of the Forestry Service in the Department of Agriculture, for supporting Glavis, public clamor for a thorough investigation swelled. After much agitation a concurrent resolution was introduced in the Senate for a joint investigation of the Interior Department and the Bureau of Forestry. The resolution passed the Senate and went to the House, where it was generally assumed that Speaker Cannon would appoint House investigators favorable to the Administration. But Norris acted to thwart Cannon's unrestricted appointive power.[11]

Norris convinced the House that a fair investigating committee must not be designated by the Speaker. To the consternation of the Republican regulars, Norris moved to strike out of the pending resolution the words "appointed by the Speaker" and substitute "elected by the House." The Norris amendment, supported by Republican insurgents and Democrats, carried by the narrow margin of three votes. Cannon had suffered a severe rebuff and the insurgents had gained their first real victory.[12] Norris had succeeded in placing on the investigating committee names which never would have appeared on any slate selected by Cannon. The committee, however, despite the incisive efforts of Louis D. Bran-

[11] Alpheus Thomas Mason, *Bureaucracy Convicts Itself: The Ballinger-Pinchot Controversy of 1910* (New York: The Viking Press, 1941), p. 16.
[12] U.S., *Congressional Record*, 61st Cong., 2d sess. (January 7, 1910), Vol. 45, pt. 1, pp. 390, 404.

deis, cleared Ballinger. But public opinion forced him into retirement in March 1911.

On St. Patrick's Day, 1910, Norris took advantage of an unusual parliamentary situation and precipitated the struggle which stripped "Czar Cannon" of his arbitrary parliamentary power. Cannon had ruled that a census bill was privileged under the Constitution and as such could be considered out of the regular calendar order. Norris gained the floor and, skillfully utilizing the device of constitutional privilege, presented a resolution which would have the House rather than the Speaker appoint the powerful Rules Committee. Representative John Dalzell of Pennsylvania, a Cannon henchman, immediately raised a point of order against the Norris resolution, and the extended struggle began. Cannon, aware that not enough of the party faithful were present in Washington to defeat the coalition of insurgents and Democrats, began a series of dilatory tactics, hoping to delay the vote. The regulars offered a series of compromises but the insurgents refused to accept them. At one of the conferences between the insurgents and the Democrats, Champ Clark, Democratic floor leader, and his whip, Oscar Underwood, persuaded Norris to accept a compromise version of his original resolution. Norris reluctantly agreed and submitted an amendment to the resolution. When the final vote on the amended Norris resolution came, the combined insurgent-Democratic forces overrode the Cannon-led regular Republicans.[13]

Writing of the results of Norris' successful alteration of the House rules, Kenneth Hechler states:

But the most significant of all was the tremendous impetus that the Insurgent victory gave to the entire progressive movement, an impetus that can never be measured by a studious analysis of legislative procedure within the House of Representatives. Cannonism was a great symbol of reactionary tyranny, and when the blasts of Norris' trumpet felled its walls the Insurgents were spurred to press forward with the balance of their progressive program.[14]

[13] Hechler, *op. cit.*, p. 72. Hechler provides some interesting comment on the meeting between Norris and the Democrats and also discusses the changes in the resolution. Although Norris acknowledged that the new rules adopted after the Cannon battle were an improvement, nonetheless still dissatisfied, he subsequently introduced a resolution to strip the Speaker of his power to appoint standing committees. Lief, *op. cit.*, p. 107. *Cong. Record*, 61st Cong., 2d sess. (March 19, 1910), Vol. 45, pt. 4, p. 3436.
[14] Hechler, *op. cit.*, p. 82.

By the beginning of 1910 it had become evident that progressivism was destined to become as powerful a political force as Populism had been. Within the Republican party the rising progressive attitude had been articulated in President Roosevelt's 1908 Annual Message, publicized during the following year in a program calling for broad federal economic and social regulation, and reached its peak in June 1910 when Roosevelt delivered an address in which he declared that "property [is] subject to the general right of the community to regulate its use to whatever degree the public welfare may require." [15] The progressives within the Republican party were now certain that they could no longer accept Taft's complacent conservative leadership. The November elections confirmed the progressive mood and also exposed the wide breach within the Republican party between the insurgents and the regulars. The insurgents swept the Midwest and West like a wind-driven prairie fire. Wisconsin, Michigan, Indiana, and all the Republican states west of the Mississippi except the four mountain states were now in the insurgent fold. The Democrats captured the House and elected to state offices men of the stature of Woodrow Wilson, Franklin D. Roosevelt, Ben Lindsey, and Brand Whitlock. Capitalizing on the progressive mood, Senator Robert M. La Follette of Wisconsin, the very personification of progressive attitudes, took the initiative in organizing the National Progressive Republican League, which officially came into being in January 1911.[16]

The League's Declaration of Principles announced the object of the League to be "the promotion of popular government and progressive legislation" and protested that "under existing conditions legislation in the public interest has been baffled and defeated." [17] Senator Jonathan Bourne, Jr., of Oregon was elected president, and in recognition of his services on behalf of the House insurgents, Representative Norris was elected a vice-president along with Governor Chase Osborn of Michigan. The stage was

[15] Arthur S. Link, *Woodrow Wilson and the Progressive Era: 1910–1917* (New York: Harper and Brothers, 1954), pp. 19–20.
[16] Howard P. Nash, Jr., *Third Parties in American Politics* (Washington, D.C.: Public Affairs Press, 1959), p. 231. Nye, *op. cit.*, p. 260. Robert M. La Follette, *A Personal Narrative of Political Experiences* (Madison: University of Wisconsin Press, 1961), pp. 211–12.
[17] La Follette, *Personal Narrative, op. cit.*, p. 212.

being set for an intercine feud such as the GOP had not suffered since 1884.[18]

The Republican party in Nebraska, as elsewhere, was rent by factionalism. Norris, running as a progressive Republican, defeated the regular Republican, incumbent Senator Norris Brown, for the party's senatorial nomination. The party situation was further confused when the newly formed Progressive party also endorsed Norris, who had repudiated Taft. In the November senatorial preference race (popular election of Senators under the Seventeenth Amendment did not become effective until May 31, 1913), Norris defeated his old Democratic adversary, Shallenberger.[19] A Democrat, John H. Morehead, was the successful gubernatorial candidate and Woodrow Wilson won the state's electoral votes over Taft and Roosevelt.

The presidential campaign of 1912 demonstrated that the challenges and problems of industrialization and urbanization were to be resolved in the political arena. The four parties and their candidates — Republican Taft, Democrat Wilson, Bull Mooser Roosevelt, and Socialist Debs — reflected the existing shades of political sentiment. All, however, proclaimed their progressivism; even Taft would have denied that he was a conservative. The disruption within the GOP gave the Democrats control not only of the presidency but also of Congress. Norris began his Senate career as Wilson inaugurated the New Freedom.

SON OF A WILD JACKASS

On January 22, 1913, the Nebraska legislature, in accordance with the mandate of the state's voters, elected George W. Norris

[18] Charles Crane of Chicago, a wealthy liberal industrialist, was elected treasurer and Frederic C. Howe was elected secretary. The executive committee included Senators Clapp and Bristow, Congressmen Hubbard, Lenroot, and Kent. Others associated with the League included: Senators Brown of Nebraska, Cummins of Iowa, Gronna of North Dakota, Dixon of Montana; Governors Aldrich of Nebraska, Carey of Wyoming, Hiram Johnson of California, McGovern of Wisconsin, and Stubbs of Kansas; William U'Ren, William Allen White, Ray Stannard Baker, Louis Brandeis, and the Pinchots. Lief, *op. cit.*, p. 113. Norris also sponsored a branch League in Nebraska. Neuberger and Kahn, *op. cit.*, p. 42. Nye, *op. cit.*, p. 261.
[19] For a thorough discussion of the turbulent party situation in Nebraska during this period, see Lowitt, *Making of a Progressive, op. cit.*, pp. 216–69.

senator. During his first term in the Senate, he battled to amend the Underwood Tariff, urged a graduated income tax, proposed a conservation measure (Raker bill), and called for several investigations. He also vigorously led the opposition to Attorney General McReynolds' appointment to the Supreme Court, arguing that McReynolds was pro–big business, and secured the adoption of a resolution calling for an investigation of the primary campaign expenses of Senators Boies Penrose of Pennsylvania and Roger Sullivan of Illinois. As a result of this investigation, in great public indignation, Norris bolted the party and actively campaigned in Pennsylvania for Penrose's opponent, Progressive Gifford Pinchot. This action caused the staid *New York Times* to editorialize, "We recall no case in which a Senator has gone into another state to oppose the candidate of his own party. It requires a high degree of courage." [20]

Senator Norris attracted national attention as a radical Republican in party matters and as an articulate opponent of Woodrow Wilson's foreign policy. The Nebraskan helped in filibustering to death the Administration's Armed Ship bill. Wilson, exceedingly distressed at this setback, branded the obstructionists "a little group of willful men" who "had rendered the great government of the United States helpless and contemptible." When events inexorably led Wilson to request that Congress declare war, Norris was one of six in the Senate who voted against the war resolution and thereby exposed himself to national calumny and possible political extinction.[21]

Deeply disturbed by the criticism engendered by his pacifist stand, Norris seriously considered retiring from public life. Nonetheless, he filed for renomination in the spring of 1918, won the primary, and in the general election defeated Democrat John H. Morehead.[22]

[20] *New York Times*, Oct. 22, 1914, 10:2.
[21] The filibusterers, in addition to Norris, were: William Joel Stone of Missouri, Robert M. La Follette of Wisconsin, Asle J. Gronna of North Dakota, William F. Kirby of Arkansas, Harry Lane of Oregon, James K. Vardaman of Mississippi, Albert B. Cummins of Iowa, James A. O'Gorman of New York, and William S. Kenyon of Iowa. See Chapter Five for Norris' views on foreign affairs.
[22] Norris, *Fighting Liberal, op. cit.*, p. 202. Winton Henry Beaven, *A Critical Analysis and Appraisal of the Public Address of Senator George W. Norris* (Ann Arbor: University Microfilms, 1950, Publication No. 1947), p. 45.

From the signing of the Armistice through the Depression, Senator Norris was one of the foremost gadflies in the articulate and irreverent Senate group which came to be known as "Sons of the Wild Jackass." [23] "The Wild Jackasses" constantly opposed the Republican administrations of Harding, Coolidge, and Hoover and were largely responsible for keeping alive the spirit of progressivism.

The election of 1920 bellwethered significant and substantial changes in American foreign and domestic policy. The idealism of the previous two decades, now largely spent, could not halt the dismal trend toward insularity and Babbitt-like complacency. America rejected membership in the League of Nations and the reforms associated with the progressive movement ceased. "America's present need," Warren Gamaliel Harding pontificated ungrammatically to an applauding audience in May 1920, "is not heroics, but healing; not nostrums, but normalcy; not revolution, but restoration . . . not surgery, but serenity." [24] Although in the early twenties the progressive movement had been broken by the war, it slowly began to recover. After the election of 1920, fearing that reaction might triumph permanently, Norris was one of a small group of congressmen who met to establish the People's Legislative Service. The farm depression of 1921 provided the background for the successful efforts of the People's Legislative Service and in the elections of 1922, a number of midwestern and western progressive Republicans were elected to the Sixty-eighth Congress. Noting the heartening progressive trend in the election, Senator Robert M. La Follette of Wisconsin, acting for the PLS, sent out a form letter suggesting "that the time is opportune for a conference to discuss a definite plan for the cooperation of all the Progressives in Congress." [25]

Under La Follette's urging a Progressive Conference convened

[23] Senator George Higgins Moses of New Hampshire on November 7, 1929, during an address to a meeting of New England manufacturers, described the bloc of progressive senators who had been plaguing the Administration as "Sons of the Wild Jackass." Ray Tucker and Frederick R. Barkley, *Sons of the Wild Jackass* (Boston: L. C. Page and Company, 1932), p. v.

[24] Wesley M. Bagby, *The Road to Normalcy: The Presidential Campaign and Election of 1920* (Baltimore: The Johns Hopkins Press, 1962), p. 23.

[25] Robert M. La Follette to George W. Norris, November 18, 1922, George W. Norris Papers, Manuscripts Division, Library of Congress (hereafter cited as Norris Papers). Nash, *op. cit.*, p. 276.

in Washington on December 1 and 2, 1922. Norris, elected chairman, promptly emphasized that the new bloc was not to be considered a third party;[26] it had been organized for nonpartisan legislative effort: "To drive special privilege out of control of government and restore it to the people."[27]

Norris' action in emphasizing the nonpartisan character of the conference was in keeping with his party independence. Even before the affable and shallow Warren G. Harding became President, on January 5, 1921, Norris had displayed his independence when he proposed to reduce the size of the appropriation for Harding's inaugural ceremonies, an action hardly calculated to endear him to the party faithful.[28] He had been equally indiscreet politically when he had characterized the Newberry election in Michigan as the auction of a Senate seat. "The sale was public," he stated in the Senate, "the bidding was in the open, and the property was knocked down to the highest bidder."[29] This was followed a month later by the blast that "there is no doubt the country is tired of the Republican Party."[30] When asked if he had any regrets for having criticized the Administration, he replied that "he had no occasion for apologizing for anything."[31]

Norris was exceedingly reluctant to seek renomination for a third term in the Senate. To his astonishment, his name was placed in nomination despite him, however.[32] When unhappy Republican stalwarts in Nebraska threatened to drop him from the ticket because of his anti-party sentiments,[33] Norris challenged the state Republican Committee to read him out of the party and offered to submit to a second primary. But the challenge of a second primary was not accepted. The *New York Times*, in a fit of pique declared:

Whether his name stays on the ballot or not, it has no business there. Every vote he gets as a Republican candidate is a vote obtained by false pretenses. The disintegration of parties is one of the gravest

[26] Norris to B. Brewer, December 8, 1922, Norris Papers.
[27] *New York Times*, December 3, 1922, 2:1.
[28] *Ibid.*, January 6, 1921, 3:5.
[29] For Norris' account of the Newberry election, see "A Senate Seat for Sale," *Fighting Liberal, op. cit. Cong. Record*, 67th Cong., 2d sess. (January 11, 1922), Vol. 62, pt. 1, p. 1052.
[30] *New York Times*, February 15, 1921, 12:1.
[31] Norris to C. O. Talmage, July 24, 1924, Norris Papers.
[32] Tucker and Barkley, *op. cit.*, p. 52.
[33] *New York Times*, May 12, 1924, 9:2.

troubles in the United States. The best thing that Nebraska could do is elect a "straight" Democratic Senator. That is impossible. If the Republicans who are trying to beat Norris fail, they will at least have done what they could for the restoration of party responsibility and responsible government by means of parties.[34]

But Nebraska returned Norris to Washington. Although not in favor of the organization of a third party, Norris supported his friend Robert M. La Follette in his 1924 race for the presidency; but he made no attack upon any of the candidates on the Republican ticket.[35]

Soon after his unsuccessful bid for the presidency, Senator La Follette died. In the popular mind Senator Norris became the titular head of the Progressive party. Norris was extremely distressed about this because he believed it was improper for him to "assume the leadership of any party or faction." Nonetheless, he proclaimed his willingness to work with anyone, regardless of party affiliation, "if he believes in the same progressive principles of government." [36]

Senator Norris further estranged himself from the Republican organization and the Administration when he attacked the candidacy of wealthy Republican William B. Vare in his 1926 race for a Pennsylvania Senate seat. Charging that excessive monies had been spent to secure the nomination, Norris strongly urged the election of Vare's Democratic opponent, William B. Wilson. Despite Norris' support of Wilson, the strong Republican machine in Pennsylvania succeeded in electing Vare to the Senate. Not content to permit the issue to die quietly, Norris successfully persuaded the Senate that Vare should be denied his seat.[37]

During 1927 Norris' name was frequently mentioned as a presidential possibility and in 1928 the insurgents in the Northwest started a Norris boom to nominate him as Republican presidential candidate. The Senator tried to discourage these efforts, even after

[34] *Ibid.*, November 6, 1924, 2:3.
[35] *Ibid.*, September 28, 1924, 3:1.
[36] Norris to Warren Shaw Fisher, July 2, 1925, Norris Papers.
[37] George W. Norris, "The Pennsylvania Patriot's Duty: Elect a Democrat," *The Nation*, CXXIII (July 14, 1926), 28. For the debate between Norris and James M. Beck of Pennsylvania, Solicitor General of the United States in the Harding and Coolidge administrations, see James M. Beck, "Can a Senator-Elect Be Denied His Seat?" *Congressional Digest*, VI (November 1927), 305–8.

WINGATE COLLEGE LIBRARY
WINGATE, N. C.

Nebraska and Wisconsin delegates were pledged to him at the Republican convention.[38] When the Republicans nominated Herbert Hoover in June of 1928, Norris grimly issued a statement that "'the action of the Republican Convention at Kansas City, both as to platform and candidate for President, will be a sad disappointment to every progressive citizen of the United States." [39]

Distressed at the choice of Hoover, Norris threw his support to the Democratic nominee, Alfred E. Smith. This required a great deal of courage; the Nebraskan's constituency was rural, dry, and Protestant, while Smith was urban, wet, and Catholic. But to Norris the fundamental question was, "Shall the great trusts, particularly the water power trust, control the destiny of our Republic?" [40] And since Smith was "right" on the fundamental question, Norris felt obliged to support him. The Senator's solid support of Smith, which he never regretted, was nonetheless to plague him in subsequent campaigns.

When Norris in 1930 ran for re-election to his fourth term in the Senate he was subjected to the hardest and most acrimonious campaign in his career. Conservative Republicans induced the manager of the Skaggs Safeway store of Broken Bow, Nebraska, coincidentally named George W. Norris, to run in the Republican primaries, defeating the Norris campaign before it had a chance to get underway.

The Norris faction, however, succeeded in eliminating Grocer Norris' name from the primary ballot. The Republican National Committee then began to flood Nebraska with scurrilous campaign literature. There were charges that Norris was a drunkard and an immoral wretch; in the KKK regions it was rumored that the Senator's wife was a Catholic. A fictitious letter purporting to be from a Tammany committeeman to a Democrat in Nebraska urged him to vote for Norris because he was a good Democrat. But despite the abuse and vilification, Norris won over Gilbert M. Hitchcock, Democratic nominee and owner of the Omaha *World Herald*.[41]

[38] Beaven, *op. cit.*, p. 63. Prior to the Farmer-Labor convention Norris had received the endorsement of the La Follette Progressive Platform Conferees in January of 1928. *New York Times,* January 22, 1928, 26:8.
[39] *Ibid.*, June 3, 1928, 3:3. Statement of George W. Norris, June 16, 1928, Norris Papers.
[40] Norris to Oswald Garrison Villard, June 19, 1928, Norris Papers.
[41] Beaven, *op. cit.*, p. 73.

After Norris' re-election, Charles S. Ryckman, editor of the Fremont (Nebraska) *Tribune*, in a spirit of conservative rebellion — like that which had motivated William Allen White's celebrated editorial "What's the Matter with Kansas?" in the Emporia *Gazette* some years before — wrote an editorial which won the 1930 Pulitzer Prize. The Ryckman thesis was that "the State of Nebraska has elected Norris to the United States Senate . . . mainly because he is not wanted there."

Nebraska nurses an ingrowing grouch against America in general and eastern America in particular. The state expects nothing from the national government, which it regards as largely under eastern control, and asks nothing . . . if Norris were forced to rely upon what he has done in Congress for Nebraska, he would approach election day with fear in his heart. But Senator Norris has found another way to serve Nebraska. By making himself objectionable to federal administrations without regard to political complexion and to eastern interests of every kind, he has afforded Nebraskans a chance to vent their wrath. He is, perhaps unwittingly, an instrument of revenge. . . . The explanation of this fascinating political paradox is to be found not in an analysis of Norris, but of Nebraska. As a Senator, Norris has given Nebraska something the state never had before. He has put the "Gentleman from Nebraska" on the front page in America and kept him there. . . . The summary of all is that Nebraska derives a great deal of pleasure out of shoving George Norris down the great American throat . . . Nebraska gets the same amusement out of his antics that a small boy gets out of sicing a dog on an alley cat. . . .

Ryckman further pointed out that there was an instinctive resentment on the part of the people of the states between the Mississippi and the mountains "against the failure of the far east to understand and appreciate the middle west." Norris was being returned to the Senate in a spirit that was vindictive and retaliatory. He was "the burr Nebraska delights in putting under the eastern saddle." [42]

Norris was deeply hurt by Ryckman's analysis. "The Ryckman editorial," he wrote to another Pulitzer Prize winner, historian Claude Bowers, "is a direct insult to the people of the State of Nebraska." [43] It was "another illustration of the terrible bitterness of special interests." [44] The condemnation contained in the edi-

[42] Charles S. Ryckman, "The Gentleman from Nebraska," Pulitzer Prize Editorial of 1930.
[43] Norris to Claude Bowers, May 21, 1931, Norris Papers.
[44] Norris to Edwin C. Wiggenhorn, May 19, 1931, Norris Papers.

torial, however, did not stop him from continuing his activities in behalf of the progressive cause.

After the 1930 mid-term election, and as the Depression worsened, the League for Independent Political Action launched an experiment designed to induce the progressives in Congress to lend support to the movement for a new party. Donald R. McCoy has pointed out that "the League devised the strategy of trying first to convert the leading congressional progressive, Norris, hoping that his colleagues would follow him." [45] Just before Christmas, John Dewey wrote to Norris and reminded him of the shabby treatment which he had recently received at the hands of the Republican party and called on him "to sever forever your connection with that political machine and form with those in the League for Independent Political Action and other liberal groups a new party to which you can give your full allegiance. . . ." Dewey stressed that Norris stood for social planning and control and argued that it was logical for Norris to renounce both of the old parties and "help give birth to a new party based upon the principle of planning and control for the purpose of building happier lives." Dewey prophesied that a liberal party representing the interests of the people would win the presidency by 1940.[46]

Norris rejected Dewey's proposal; the solution was not another party, but rather to make democracy more representative by abolishing the electoral college and permitting the people to vote directly for the President. "I think," replied Norris, "experience has shown that the people will not respond to a demand for a new party except in case of a great emergency where there is practically a political revolution." [47] Dewey was disgusted with Norris and said so. He charged that the progressives in Congress were impractical in thinking that they were ever going to achieve anything of importance if they failed to face the fundamental issue of whether the people or the plutocrats were to control the government.[48]

Immediately after the Dewey-Norris correspondence had been made public, Congressman Will R. Wood of Indiana, chairman of the Republican Congressional Committee, accused Norris of

[45] Donald R. McCoy, *Angry Voices: Left-of-Center Politics in the New Deal Era* (Lawrence: University of Kansas Press, 1958), p. 8.
[46] John Dewey to Norris, December 23, 1930, Norris Papers.
[47] Norris to John Dewey, December 1930, Norris Papers.
[48] McCoy, *op. cit.*, p. 9.

being a demagogue and a political chameleon. Wood charged
Norris with planning to support Governor Franklin D. Roosevelt
in the forthcoming presidential election. Norris categorically denied Wood's accusation, but then hedged by stating to reporters
that although he would not say whom he would support in the
coming national election, "Roosevelt was the best man to fight
the power trust." [49]

After having equivocated on this point, Norris, along with Senators Cutting, Wheeler, Costigan, and La Follette, Jr., called a
Conference of Progressives which was held in Washington, D.C.,
on March 11 and 12, 1931.[50] In his opening address, Norris, as
chairman of the committee of Senators who had called the Conference, pointed out that the committee "was not moved by any
personal ambition or by any desire or intention of furthering the
candidacy of any man or set of men to gain political favor or by
any desire to advance the interests of any political party." [51]

The purpose of the Conference was to outline a program of con-
structive legislation dealing with certain economic and political
conditions for presentation to the first session of the Seventy-sec-
ond Congress. Round-table discussions were held on such subjects
as unemployment, agriculture, industrial stabilization, and public
utilities. Norris, by this time, was firmly convinced that it would
be impossible for the progressives to control the forthcoming Republican convention, although he still professed that "the progressives are in a majority in the rank and file of the Republican
Party." [52]

Before the Democratic convention met Norris declared himself
for Franklin D. Roosevelt, and when FDR received the nomination
Norris vigorously endorsed him.[53] In September 1932, Norris ac-

[49] *New York Times*, December 29, 1930, 1:4.
[50] *Ibid.*, November 24, 1931, 2:5.
[51] Conference of Progressives, *Proceedings* (Washington, March 11 and 12,
1931), p. 7. All the contributors to this conference were oldtime progressives.
The costs were covered by Norris, Jonathan Bourne, Amos Pinchot, Judson
Welliver, Edward P. Costigan, and Cornelia Bryce Pinchot. See Bankbook
of Progressive Conference, Norris Papers.
[52] Norris to Edward J. Jeffries, March 23, 1931, Norris Papers.
[53] *New York Times*, May 6, 1932, 3:2. Norris statement to Paramount News,
reprinted in *Cong. Record*, 72d Cong., 1st sess. (July 7, 1932), Vol. 75, pt.
13, p. 14738. When asked by a college student why he was not supporting
Socialist candidate Norman Thomas, whose latest books *As I See It* and
America's Way Out "would indicate that his ideas are more in accord with

cepted the honorary chairmanship of the National Progressive League for Roosevelt. Beginning his campaign for FDR with an article ironically entitled "Why I Am a Better Republican than President Hoover," he bitingly condemned Hoover for being wrong on every vital issue confronting the nation.[54] The League adopted Norris' slogan, "What this country needs is another Roosevelt in the White House," but Norris made it quite clear that the Progressive League for Roosevelt would be strictly nonpartisan and that he would reserve complete freedom of action in the Senate. Norris hoped that the "progressive philosophy of government and its objectives" would be constantly kept before the country.[55]

PERFECT GENTLE KNIGHT

After the years of arid Republican domination, Norris welcomed the coming of the New Deal. He was, in general, an enthusiastic supporter of FDR's policies and was willing to permit experimental stopgap legislation. In a 1935 interview with *New York Times* correspondent Ray Tucker, the Nebraskan declared that he had no regrets in having cast his political lot with FDR because "the last two years . . . produced more social legislation for the common man" than any two since he had come to Washington.[56]

But Norris did not embrace Roosevelt's desire to build a tight Democratic political organization. Norris and other progressives were shocked and distressed by the treatment accorded Bronson Cutting, the progressive Republican senator from New Mexico, by the Democratic national organization. Despite the effective support Cutting had given to Roosevelt in 1932 and to most of the features of the New Deal, the Democratic hierarchy endorsed his Democratic opponent, Dennis Chavez, a machine politician. Cutting retained his seat by a narrow margin and the Democrats

your own progressive sentiments than even those of Roosevelt," Norris replied that there was a great deal of difference between Hoover and Roosevelt, and that Thomas as a third-party candidate would not stand a chance of being elected. Chester Hart to Norris, August 1932; Norris to Chester Hart, August 20, 1932, Norris Papers.

[54] *Liberty*, September 24, 1932, pp. 13–16.
[55] *New York Times*, February 26, 1933, 1:5.
[56] Ray Tucker, "Norris Surveys the Political Scene," *New York Times Magazine*, July 14, 1935, p. 3.

contested the vote. On his return East from one of the subsequent election hearings, Cutting was killed in an airplane crash. Chavez was appointed to succeed him in the Senate.

When Chavez was conducted down the aisle to take the oath of office, Senators Norris, Hiram Johnson, La Follette, Jr., Nye, and Shipstead departed in protest. Borah, who was absent, declared that if he had been present he would have done the same thing. "I left the Chamber," Norris emphasized, "because it was the only way, in my helplessness, that I could show my condemnation of the disgraceful and unwarranted fight made to drive Senator Cutting out of public office. The determined opposition of the Democratic National Committee and its chairman to bring about the defeat of Senator Cutting is the greatest case of ingratitude in history. It is a blot upon the record of the administration." Norris later sided with Huey Long when the Kingfish called for an investigation of the political activities of James A. Farley, Roosevelt's chief patronage dispenser and Postmaster General.[57]

Despite his occasional disagreements with the Administration, Norris again supported FDR in 1936, and FDR, in turn, spoke for Norris in Nebraska. At Chicago, on September 11, 1936, the Progressive National Committee Supporting Franklin D. Roosevelt for President elected Norris its honorary chairman. In a ringing endorsement of FDR the Nebraskan affirmed, "We love him for the enemies he has made, and we should give him our undivided support, in order that he may carry to a successful conclusion the war against oppression and injustice." [58]

But Norris also had to think about his own renomination and re-election to the Senate. The campaign of 1930 still a bitter memory, he again decided to retire. Once more his friends implored him to run and he once more refused.[59] Norris had no desire to be the candidate of a party whose state and national leaders had undertaken to steal an election by imposing a dummy candidate; yet under no circumstance would he have been willing to accept a Democratic nomination.[60] In response to nominating petitions,

[57] McCoy, *op. cit.*, pp. 69–70.
[58] George W. Norris, Statement to the Conference of Progressives at the Morrison Hotel, Chicago, September 11, 1936, Norris Papers.
[59] Oswald Garrison Villard, "Pillars of Government: George W. Norris," *Forum*, XCV (April 1936), 249.
[60] *New York Times*, November 16, 1935, 1:4. *Fighting Liberal, op. cit.*, p. 369.

circulated largely through the efforts of James E. Lawrence, editor of the Lincoln *Star*, Norris decided to run as an Independent.

The Nebraska campaign of 1936 was conducted against a bleak background. Not only had the Depression wracked the countryside, but the crops had been seared by drought and ravaged by "black blizzards." People by the thousands were leaving the state. The fight for the Senate seat became a three-ring circus. The Republicans ran Robert Simmons, an ex-congressman with no particular qualifications; Terry Carpenter, later to reappear with sundry other political labels, ran as a nominal Democratic candidate, although Norris had received FDR's blessings as well as support from Arthur Mullen, the Omaha political boss. Carpenter waged an aggressive campaign in which he appealed to the Coughlinites, the Townsendites, and the Share-the-Wealthers.[61] (Ironically, an embittered Al Smith, who had benefited in 1928 because of Norris' independence, now came to Nebraska to campaign against Norris and denounce Roosevelt for "betraying" the Democratic party by his support of Norris' Independent candidacy.) In a vigorous speech praising Norris, President Roosevelt insisted:

George Norris' candidacy transcends state and party lines. In our national history we have had few elder statesmen who like him have preserved the aspirations of youth as they accumulated the wisdom of years. He is one of the major prophets of America . . . Nebraska will be doing a great service, not only to itself but to every other State in the Union and to the Nation as a whole if it places this great American above partisanship and keeps George Norris in the Senate of the United states.[62]

Yet despite FDR's appeal to the voters of Nebraska, Norris, in a race in which over a half a million votes were cast, won by only a little more than 35,000. Simmons, the Republican, indicating a trend which would become more strongly apparent in the next election, came in a close second.

But now many of Roosevelt's former progressive allies became dissatisfied with the Administration's policies. In April of 1938, at the urging of the La Follette brothers of Wisconsin — Governor Phillip La Follette and Senator Robert La Follette, Jr.— the National Progressives of America was established as the nucleus of a new third party. Norris, by now the elder statesman of American

[61] Beaven, *op. cit.*, p. 96.
[62] Statement of Franklin D. Roosevelt at Omaha, Nebraska, October 10, 1936.

progressivism, disassociated himself from this new movement and expressed the fear that the new organization might split the liberal forces. Indeed, Herbert Hoover expressed the hope that the newly formed National Progressives would be a divisive element in the New Deal coalition and thereby aid the Republicans' return to power.[63]

As the 1940 elections drew near and foreign policy began to play an increasingly important role in domestic politics, Norris was urged by many to desert Roosevelt.[64] But Norris rejected this idea and accepted the honorary chairmanship of the National Committee of Independent Voters for Roosevelt and Wallace.

The Nebraskan strongly believed that all liberals should unite and support FDR in his bid for a third term.[65] Norris bitterly opposed the Republican candidate and warned that if Wendell Willkie were elected President "monopoly and human greed would soon be in control of governmental activities." [66]

After the 1940 elections had returned Roosevelt to the White House, Norris' activities in the Senate began to wane. Not only was he advancing in years, but external affairs had preempted the issues on which he was strongest. Nevertheless, he took a great interest in the operations of the selective service system and made a number of speeches in which he pointed out the need for keeping as many men on the farms as possible. After Pearl Harbor and America's entrance into World War II, Norris advocated the establishment of a separate government authority for making synthetic

[63] McCoy, *op. cit.*, pp. 167–72.
[64] For example, Oswald Garrison Villard wrote Norris, "Some of us liberals who are as staunch in our faith as ever we were, believe the re-election of the President will mean war inevitably and then complete dictatorship." Oswald Garrison Villard to Norris, September 24, 1940, Norris Papers.
[65] Previously Norris had declared his opposition to any President running for a third term and during the 1940 campaign his words returned to haunt him. He rationalized his new position, however: ". . . the objections to a third term fade into insignificance when we realize, first, that he [President Roosevelt] had no ambitions to be a dictator, and second, that under the present existing emergency it would be unsafe to replace him with an untried leader . . . after all, what is the objection to a third term, so long as the people are free to vote as they please? If the man to be chosen for a third term is himself free from the objection that he is trying to make himself a dictator; if he wants to preserve in full, without any limitation, the right of the people to write, speak, act, and vote as they see fit, then there can be no danger, if such a man were elected for a third term." *New York Times*, September 28, 1940, 12:2.
[66] Norris to W. A. Brownlee, September 21, 1940, Norris Papers.

rubber from agricultural and forest products. He was active also in promoting the passage of the anti–poll tax bill; so much so that he reported the bill on behalf of the Judiciary Committee.[67]

The Senator battled to the last what he considered to be corruption in the political process. He conducted a one-man campaign against FDR's nomination for a federal judgeship of Thomas F. Meaney, a Boss Hague henchman. In a three-hour speech he blasted the Hague machine as "one of the most disreputable and demagogic organizations that ever existed." [68]

George W. Norris' fifth senatorial term came to a close in 1942 and he agreed to run as an Independent. FDR again vigorously supported him, but Norris, now an octogenarian, did not conduct much of a campaign. He remained in Washington until the Friday preceding the election, trying to push through the passage of the anti–poll tax legislation. The race was again a three-way contest: Norris the Independent, Kenneth S. Wherry the Republican, and Foster May the Democrat. In a statement to the voters of Nebraska, Norris indicated that he was going to campaign solely on his record. "If in the coming campaign," he declared, "I should be defeated, I would feel that in effect it was a repudiation from my own people of all of my forty years of service." [69] Wherry made the new Deal his sole issue and defeated Norris by a large majority.

In an eight-page single-spaced letter to Harold Ickes, a shocked and embittered Norris attempted to explain his defeat. Nebraskans, he surmised, were tired of his support of the New Deal and voted to remove him from the Senate, not because they had anything against him personally, but because they disliked the New Deal. "There seems to be a universal hatred among a lot of our people against Roosevelt. . . . In the campaign nothing was said by the opposition against me. Even my two opponents when they mentioned me or referred to me, did it with praise and commendation." [70] But Norris was understandably bitter. "The most important thing," he commented, "is that righteousness has been crucified and the people I love have condemned the things I held most sacred; personally I find it a repudiation of forty years of serv-

[67] Norris, *Fighting Liberal, op. cit.*, p. 362.
[68] *Time*, XL (July 13, 1942), 15.
[69] Norris, *Fighting Liberal, op. cit.*, p. 370. Statement by George W. Norris, n.d., Norris Papers.
[70] Norris to Harold Ickes, n.d., Norris Papers.

ice." [71] "Nebraska was tired of me," he wrote in anguish and humiliation to his old friend Carl Marsh.[72]

Following the repudiation at the polls, Senator and Mrs. Norris abandoned their Washington apartment and returned to their home in McCook, Nebraska. Norris' friends in Washington realized that he was now without a major source of income and suggested creating a federal job for him. Before leaving Washington, Norris was offered the position of chairman of the Tennessee Valley Board. He declined this offer even when the Attorney General, at the request of the President, urged him to accept.[73] FDR pressed him to accept a post on the Tariff Commission,[74] and Cordell Hull urged that he serve as a State Department special consultant. Now in deteriorating health, Norris realistically declined all of these offers, as well as a number of others, in favor of a contract to write his Autobiography.[75] He completed the dictation of his Autobiography, *Fighting Liberal*, eight weeks before he died on September 3, 1944.

THE GENTLEMAN FROM NEBRASKA

After Norris had been defeated in his bid for re-election to his sixth term in the Senate a number of testimonial dinners were given in his honor. Acting on the principle that it is nice to receive flowers when one can still appreciate them, a group of Norris' friends assembled in the ornate Chinese room of Washington's Mayflower Hotel to do him honor and assuage the bitterness of his defeat. William Allen White, unable to be present at the ceremonies, nonetheless captured the spirit of the occasion when he telegraphed: "I know of no other man in the United States who has done so much for his country in the last forty years as George W. Norris." [76] The sentiments expressed by the editor of the Emporia *Gazette* were patently borne out by the fact that many of the

---

[71] Washington *Daily News*, November 5, 1942, 1:7.
[72] Norris to Carl Marsh, January 4, 1943, Norris Papers.
[73] Norris to Nathan Robertson, September 23, 1944, Norris Papers.
[74] Franklin Delano Roosevelt to Norris, February 14, 1944, Norris Papers.
[75] Norris to John W. Morland, February 12, 1944, Norris Papers.
[76] "George W. Norris: Proceedings in Connection with the Testimonial Dinner Given on December 10, 1942, Washington, D.C.," *Senate Document No. 292*, 77th Congress, 2nd sess. (Washington, D.C.: Government Printing Office, 1942), p. 3.

major luminaries of American political life, as well as a host of foreign dignitaries, were willing to surrender their valuable time to do honor to a man whose political career was obviously completed.

As the speeches were delivered it grew evident why so many people had come out to attend a dinner for a man who was no longer in a position to help them. George W. Norris was *sui generis*. Through two-score years on the national political scene he had become a symbol of Parnassian integrity, and the embodiment of the progressive ideals of a vibrant democracy. But beneath this symbol were characteristics which best can be epitomized by the phrase, the Gentleman from Nebraska.

The Gentleman from Nebraska was an independent Senate giant who battled for causes which he thought necessary for the advancement of American democracy. "Senator George W. Norris," David Fellman once wrote, "was a doggedly righteous man who never stopped battling for the Lord and the common people in a world of sinful men." [77] The genesis of Norris' political career was shaped by his early life in a hard frontier community. In his Autobiography, he recalls that he received a very nominal sum as his share of his father's estate, but the money that came to him was the least of his heritage:

. . . There on that farm I lost all fear of poverty. I learned to live most simply, and I learned to get a great joy out of work. It never occurred to me in those years that the lack of money was of any consequence. I grew up to believe wholly and completely in men and women who lived simply, and frugally, and in fine faith. I learned that fear was inspired in men and women who could not reconcile themselves to the possibility that hardship and sacrifice might confront them in battling for the right. [78]

Norris' boyhood in the pioneer Ohio region inculcated in him a deep respect for justice, a great sympathy for the oppressed, and the rudiments of social vision. As a young boy he found his mother planting a seedling; knowing that she would never live to see it

[77] David Fellman, "The Liberalism of Senator Norris," *American Political Science Review*, XL (February 1946), 27. For example, Norris in submitting his article, "Hope for the Progressives," wrote to *The Nation's* editor, Oswald Garrison Villard, that he would not take an honorarium for it because "I want you to accept the article as my contribution to the Cause." Norris to Villard, December 22, 1928, Norris Papers.
[78] Norris, *Fighting Liberal, op. cit.*, p. 8.

bear fruit, he asked why she exerted such effort on something from which she would never benefit. His mother replied that while she would never see the tree bear fruit, someone else would. Norris learned then that one plants not only for the present but also for the future.[79] His mother also communicated to him a fear of debt and a sense of puritanical righteousness which remained with him throughout his life. He grew up in straitened financial circumstances and was later fond of recalling that he ate his first ice cream cone on his twenty-first birthday. Even as a senator he often wondered how it would feel to walk "into a restaurant and order a first-class meal without looking at the prices on the menu card." [80] His college education was paid for by his own earnings and at Valparaiso, a poor man's school; his spirit of democracy expanded to profoundly influence his actions.

The Middle Border years contributed to his staunch faith in democracy and a determination to help it function. There Norris acquired simplicity, frugality, and a zeal for hard work. Throughout his life the Nebraskan opposed pomp and excessive display of wealth. His sense of frugality, however, often bordered on the absurd. He spoke in the Senate with equal fervor against army expenditures for the breeding of saddle horses ("the officers of the army ought to be able to get along with common ponies,") and what he considered to be Woodrow Wilson's excessive expenditures in Europe.[81] One of the reasons for his opposition to the Townsend Plan was its provision that every beneficiary was required to spend his pension within the month. "This would have a tendency to inculcate in the minds of beneficiaries an inclination toward extravagance and would kill any spirit of economy or thrift." [82] Norris was always suspicious of those who kept their "feet under the table of the rich" and ill at ease when forced to dine "where stiff shirts and high collars, with spike tail coats, all cover up and conceal the real man." [83]

[79] *Ibid.*, p. 19.
[80] Tucker and Barkley, *op. cit.*, p. 43. *PM*, October 16, 1942, no page, Norris Scrapbook, Norris Papers.
[81] Norris charged that Wilson had spent "more money in his travels about the world than had ever before been expended in any country by any prince, potentate, or monarch, since the beginning of civilization." *Cong. Record*, 66th Cong., 1st sess. (September 10, 1919), Vol. 58, pt. 5, p. 5158.
[82] Norris to W. E. Lamb, January 18, 1935, Norris Papers.
[83] Norris to Al Fairbrother, January 28, 1928, Norris Papers.

Excessive drinking evoked in him a sense of moral revulsion. He believed that temperance was a cardinal virtue; the consumption of liquor was a dishonorable business which made "drunkards, widows and orphans." [84] But his puritanical nature was tempered by a streak of humor. Norris liked to laugh and was a master of satire and parody. During the controversy over the seating at official functions of widowed Vice-President Charles Curtis' sister and hostess, Norris, in a public letter, sardonically asked Secretary of State Henry L. Stimson to "officially determine . . . where the Vice-President's sister should sit at the table, or indeed, whether she should have any dinner." [85] And he convulsed the Senate, to the discomfiture of Vice-President Charles G. Dawes, with his parody of Sheridan's Ride.[86]

When humor was directed at him, however, he took offense. During the Muscle Shoals hearings a woman jestingly testified that when Norris had inspected Muscle Shoals in 1922 he had promised that he would support the Ford offer if he could kiss one of the girls present at a barbecue. The witness stated that he had kissed the girl and was now betraying his word. Norris took this very seriously and charged that he was being blackmailed.[87]

This sense of personal seriousness also extended to his work. It was usual for him to work extended hours, handling correspondence, doing research, and trying to prepare himself on public issues. If he was unprepared, generally he would not discuss the question. Once, when asked his views on a foreign policy issue, Norris replied that he had none, and apologized by saying that he had been concentrating on the Muscle Shoals issue to the exclusion of all other things.[88] But Norris was not all work; he loved to read.

In a letter to his old friend John F. Cordeal of McCook, with whom he had shared a law office, Norris summed up his basic philosophy: "The truth is that my religion and my politics are

[84] Norris to J. A. Morrison, November 30, 1928, Norris Papers.
[85] Norris to Henry L. Stimson, April 6, 1929, Norris Papers.
[86] *Cong. Record*, 69th Cong., Spec. sess. (March 12, 1925), Vol. 67, pt. 1, p. 150.
[87] U.S., Congress, Senate, Committee on Agriculture and Forestry, *Hearings*, 68th Cong., 1st sess. (May 3, 1924), pt. 2, p. 457.
[88] Richard L. Neuberger, "A Politician Unafraid: George W. Norris, Senator from Nebraska," *Harper's Magazine*, CLXXIII (September 1936), 542. Tucker and Barkley, *op. cit.*, p. 69.

one and the same . . . a government in its truest sense, is only a method of bringing to humanity the greatest amount of happiness and is founded, after all, upon the love of man for man." [89] From this simple faith Norris never swerved. He had merged the ethics of religion with the practice of politics and achieved a political career characterized by integrity and courage.

He followed his conscience and in doing so he displayed fortitude and a willingness to be unpopular. His vote against American participation in World War I and his support for Smith were political acts which took great courage. Felix Frankfurter was so impressed by Norris' backing of Smith that he wrote him, "Moral achievements are not dependent on votes and your espousal of the cause of Governor Smith will remain for many a long day one of the most inspiring acts of American public life." [90]

This independence of action and spirit also extended to the area of civil liberties. Norris never believed that loyalty in a democracy had to be secured by coercion. Consequently he opposed the censorship measures imposed by the government during World War I, and after the war urged the pardoning of prisoners who were incarcerated because "their only crime was the exercise of the right of free speech guaranteed in the Constitution." [91] During the height of the Red Scare, only a week after three thousand deportation warrants were served on suspected radicals, Norris reminded the Senate that "free speech and a free press are the fundamental cornerstones of every Government." [92] As far as Norris was concerned, "instead of stopping a man from making a speech on a street corner," he "would buy him another soap box and put it out on the street and tell him to go to it." [93] When the Federal Bureau of Investigation, in May 1940, conducted a series of wholesale roundups of potential subversives, Norris took to the Senate floor and lambasted J. Edgar Hoover and the FBI for using police-state methods. He opposed a bill which would have authorized the creation of a plant protection force for naval shore establishments because it would require a special police force. "A secret police in one country," Norris maintained, "will be fundamentally

[89] Norris, *Fighting Liberal, op. cit.*, p. 405.
[90] Felix Frankfurter to Norris, November 17, 1928, Norris Papers.
[91] Norris to J. M. Leyda, December 21, 1921, Norris Papers.
[92] *Cong. Record*, 66th Cong., 2d sess. (January 9, 1920), Vol. 59, pt. 2, p. 1253.
[93] *Ibid.*, p. 1259.

no different from a secret police in another. It is a weapon of dictators. It has no place in a democracy." [94] Senator Norris contended that one of the fundamental principles of human freedom is the right of free speech. He knew that any government which permanently suppresses this right cannot lay a just claim to being either free or civilized.

But as with so many other progressives, Norris' liberality failed to reject the intolerant beliefs of nativism and to perceive the continued plight of the American Negro. Norris admitted that it troubled his "conscience to prevent an immigrant from landing on our shores simply because he can neither read nor write," but nonetheless he voted for the literacy requirement because though imperfect, it was a means of keeping out "undesirable" people.[95] He endorsed the limiting Immigration Act of 1921 and the notorious National Origins Act of 1924. Whatever doubts Norris had about the national origins provisions were confined to their operational efficacy and were not concerned with their racist premises which prohibited Oriental immigration, sharply reduced all immigration, and discriminated against southern Europeans in favor of northern Europeans. He always wanted to limit southern European immigrants who, he believed, congregated "in certain localities in some of the large cities," thereby presenting problems of assimilation.[96]

While to a certain extent, Norris' acceptance of nativism may be explained by his agrarian distrust of the cities, no such explanation may be advanced for his failure to see the depressed condition of the Negro as a national problem. In September 1931, William E. B. DuBois, editor of *The Crisis*, invited various members of the Senate to comment on the future of the Negro in American politics. Norris' reply proceeded on the assumption that "a people who were liberated from bondage after years of servitude cannot be expected to at once reach the highest type" and urged educational development and nonpartisan political activity.[97] When Norris had a specific legislative opportunity to help the Negro, by voting for the anti-lynching bill in 1938, he failed to do so. His rational-

[94] *Cong. Record*, 77th Cong., 1st sess. (July 22, 1941), Vol. 87, pt. 6, p. 6241.
[95] *Ibid.*, 63d Cong., 3d sess. (December 31, 1914), Vol. 52, pt. 1, p. 802.
[96] Norris to J. F. Nelson, January 7, 1928, Norris Papers.
[97] George W. Norris, "The Future of the Negro in Politics," *The Crisis*, XXXVIII (September 1931), 298.

ization was that passage of the anti-lynching bill would resurrect painful memories of the Civil War and Reconstruction, doing more harm than good. His advocacy of the poll tax abolition bill, some years later, was an effort to protect the right to vote, not of Negroes specifically, but of all citizens.[98]

But above all, George W. Norris was a man with humility and a basic belief in the goodness of man and the decency of democracy. When some newspapermen, in February 1936, had the not too original idea of asking a number of public men what policies the Great Emancipator would have advocated if present, words were put into Lincoln's mouth praising or condemning the New Deal. But when Norris was asked, he replied, "Lincoln would be just like me. He wouldn't know what the hell to do!" [99] But the record contradicts him. Norris did know what to do. He had a vision of democracy based on simple equalitarian justice. To the end of his life he believed that "social progress, despite its setbacks, always has been upward and onward. Each reverse resulting from a reappearance of reactionary practices and thought has been followed by new peaks of enlightened social conceptions." [100] Henry A. Wallace epitomized Norris when he referred to him as belonging "to that small group of wise public men who clearly see the future and are willing to do something about it. They know that without progress there will be either revolution or the return of the human spirit to the cave." [101] George W. Norris always fought to protect the human spirit and to perfect the American political process.

[98] Norris, *Fighting Liberal, op. cit.*, p. 361.
[99] Johnson, "George William Norris," *The American Politician, op. cit.*, p. 83.
[100] Norris, *Fighting Liberal, op. cit.*, p. 406.
[101] Norris Testimonial Dinner Proceedings, *Senate Document No. 292, op. cit.*, p. 9.

☆ ☆ ☆ ☆ ☆ ☆ ☆ ☆ ☆

CHAPTER TWO

Political Democracy

☆ ☆ ☆ ☆ ☆ ☆ ☆ ☆ ☆

THE PEOPLE AND POLITICAL DEMOCRACY

For George W. Norris and other progressives the primary problem for American democracy was whether all the people or the powerful few would control the government. This fundamental concern that the oligarchical concentration of political control would inexorably result in economic oppression was simultaneously re-enforced by an almost religious belief in the virtue and wisdom of the common man. This view of populistic democracy, considerably more respectable in the days before the high-powered professional image makers, is traceable in its broadest strokes to the Jeffersonians and the Jacksonians, but it reached its fullest expression as a strong and basic intellectual current during Norris' early years in Congress, when progressivism was in its heyday.

Such divergent political prototypes as the rural folk hero William Jennings Bryan, the sophisticated urban academic Woodrow Wilson, and the ebullient Theodore Roosevelt adhered to the popular-government conception of democracy. "The great problem of legislation before us," crusader Robert M. La Follette ominously noted in his Autobiography, one of the bibliographic monuments of the progressive era, "is first for the people to resume control of the government and then to protect themselves against those who are throttling competition by the aid of the government."[1] One of the ways in which the people could control the government was through the use of mechanical and institutional devices. Norris and his fellow ideologues had an uncritical faith in the initiative, referendum, recall, a strong civil service, the direct primary, the abolition of the electoral college, the establishment of state unicameral legislatures, and sundry other reforms in the Congress and the Judiciary. Even after the doctrine of popular government became jaded, Norris' continued advocacy of greater participation by the people may be explained by his unyielding belief that beneath all great political issues was a moral issue on which the people with their innate wisdom were best qualified to decide. For Norris, the progressive dream of a dynamic Great Society could only be achieved when the popular will determined governmental policies.[2]

THE PERILS OF PARTYISM

Norris' personal experiences with party regularity were short-lived and disillusioning. The longer he remained in Congress the more he became a political maverick. As a freshman representative, he believed that the only chance for enlightened government was through the election of Republicans and that all the virtues of government were embodied in the Republican party. But he soon

[1] Robert M. La Follette, *A Personal Narrative of Political Experiences* (Madison: University of Wisconsin Press, 1961), p. 338. Bryan contended that the people were competent "to sit in judgment on every question which has arisen or which will arise, no matter how long our government will endure," and Wilson with similar egalitarian fervor had asserted that the Democratic party aimed "to set up a government in the world where the average man, the plain man, the common man, the ignorant man, the unaccomplished man, the poor man had a voice equal to the voice of anybody else in the settlement of the common affairs." Richard Hofstadter, *The Age of Reform: From Bryan to F.D.R.* (New York: Alfred A. Knopf, 1956), p. 260.

[2] For Norris the primary was just as important as the general election. "To deny to the citizen the right to select candidates and to confine his suffrage rights solely to a decision as between candidates after they have been selected," he maintained, "is, in reality, at least a partial denial of the right of suffrage." George W. Norris, "Why I Believe in the Direct Primary," *The Annals of the American Academy of Political and Social Science*, CVI (March 1923), 22.

learned otherwise. Even prior to the insurgent controversy with Speaker Joseph G. Cannon, he had begun to question unthinking adherence to party positions. He reluctantly concluded that the Republicans whom he had supported so vigorously were guilty of the same evils with which he had charged the Democrats. Not only were both parties machine-controlled, but they "often worked in perfect harmony and brotherly love." [3] The Senator once confided that if he were ever President of the United States his first official announcement would be to declare his administration entirely nonpartisan. "Of all the evils in Government," he always firmly maintained, "the greatest is partisanship." A nonpartisan administration on both state and national levels would restore the government to the people and permit real democracy. "When partisanship controls and party loyalty is the supreme test of good standing," he told the First National Conference of Popular Government, "then party is placed above country and the rights of the people are surrendered to the control of the boss." [4]

Norris' conception of nonpartisanship also implied a sacred reciprocal relationship between the representative and his constituents. Once the voters had elected a representative, in all normal circumstances, they should permit him to vote, speak, and act freely in the legislature. The representative, however, should be subject to recall or be willing to voluntarily subject his actions to his constituents for approval. Norris dramatically personified this attitude in March 1917, when he filibustered and voted against President Wilson's Armed Ship bill. After his position elicited extensive and bitter criticism, he wrote to Governor Keith Neville of Nebraska, "I have no desire to represent the people of Nebraska, either in the United States Senate or elsewhere if my official conduct is contrary to their wishes, and if I am misrepresenting them the remedy is a recall." Years later, in his Autobiography, he reiterated his philosophy:

The War Resolution, perhaps more than any other issue upon which I

---

[3] George W. Norris, *Fighting Liberal: The Autobiography of George W. Norris* (New York: The Macmillan Company, 1945), p. 96.

[4] See: George W. Norris, "Partisanship" (unpublished MS, October 17, 1932), Norris Papers. George W. Norris, "If I Were President" (unpublished MS, n.d.), p. 1, Norris Papers. George W. Norris. "A Nonpartisan Party," Address before First National Conference of Popular Government, Held at Memorial Continental Hall, Washington, D.C., December 6, 1913, *Senate Document No. 372*, 63rd Congress, 2nd sess. (Washington, D.C.: Government Printing Office, 1914), pp. 8, 4.

voted during all the years in Congress, raised the issue of what should be the attitude of a member of Congress. Should he always follow what he believed to be the majority sentiment of his district, or should he obey his own conscience even when, in doing so, it appeared he was voting against the wishes of a majority of his constituents? . . . I have thought conscience was the guide. Otherwise, a member of Congress giving weight to expressed public sentiment, becomes only an automatic machine. If that is the line of duty as a member of Congress, then Congress requires no patriotism, no education, and no courage. All a member has to do, if he does follow that which he believes to be the will of his constituency at all times, is to attempt to take such action as will bring him the most votes in the next election. . . .[5]

But while Norris was practicing and expounding party independence, there developed the antithetical doctrine of responsible government. Foremost in this movement were Woodrow Wilson, A. Lawrence Lowell, Henry Jones Ford, and Frank J. Goodnow, who took the position that democracy in the modern community must be conceived of as popular control over government rather than popular participation in government. Some years after Senator Norris died this position received formal articulation when the Committee on Political Parties of the American Political Science Association issued an extremely controversial report which noted, "An effective party system requires, first, that the parties are able to bring forth programs to which they commit themselves, and second, that the parties possess sufficient internal cohesion to carry out these programs." The report provoked rebuttal that centralized and disciplined parties would involve problems of federalism, the deterioration of compromise among competing groups, and the development of a multi-party system.[6] But Senator Norris never reasoned in such sophisticated terms. His very limited

[5] Richard L. Neuberger and Stephen B. Kahn, *Integrity: The Life of George W. Norris* (New York: Vanguard Press, 1937), p. 97. Under the Constitution congressmen are not subject to recall. Norris, willing to waive whatever constitutional rights he had, requested Governor Neville to convene the Nebraska legislature so that a law could be passed providing for a special election at which the question of his recall could be submitted to the people of the state. Neville, nonetheless, refused to act and Norris never submitted to a recall. Norris, *Fighting Liberal, op. cit.*, pp. 198–99.
[6] The literature concerning the doctrine of responsible parties is quite extensive. Of particular interest are: Austin Ranney, *The Doctrine of Responsible Party Government* (Urbana: University of Illinois Press, 1954). E. E. Schattschneider, *Party Government* (New York: Rinehart and Company, Inc., 1942). *Toward a More Responsible Two-Party System*, Report of the Committee on Political Parties of the American Political Science Association (New York: Rinehart and Company, Inc., 1950), pp. 17–18.

conception of the party system, furthermore, never included any insight into the inherent institutional conflict between the President and Congress, the function of parties in the management of succession to power, sectional and local conflict within the parties, effects of one-party states, or the relationship of pressure groups to the parties. Despite his many years in Washington, Norris always saw the party simply as a corrupt political machine which perpetuated itself by securing advantage and patronage for its adherents.

THE CIVIL SERVICE

Norris' extreme distrust of political parties, however, was not merely negative; it found positive expression in his continuous advocacy of strong civil service laws. His active opposition to the spoils system was, to a large extent, a reflection of his own experience. He grew up during the Era of the Great Barbecue and came to Congress when the muckraking-reform fervor was at its height. His maiden speech to the House of Representatives was a paean to the merit system, in which he declared that he was "thoroughly imbued with the idea of the righteousness of the Civil Service Law." After the insurgent controversy with President Taft and the party regulars, Norris was denied patronage; but unlike most politicians, he considered it a relief to be freed of the "onerous responsibility" of dispensing patronage.[7]

One of the Senator's favorite themes was removing the postal system from politics. He failed to accept the logic which allowed that "the postmastership in a distant town be changed because there has been a change in the White House." Well aware that postmasters and other government employees were expected to contribute to party coffers, he constantly fought for the extension and improvement of civil service in the agencies which he helped to create. When framing legislation for the establishment of the Tennessee Valley Authority and the Rural Electrification Administration, he insisted that appointments, tenure of service, promotion, and like matters be based on ability and efficiency.[8]

[7] U.S., *Congressional Record*, 58th Cong., 2d sess. (January 13, 1904), Vol. 38, pt. 1, p. 728. Norris, *Fighting Liberal, op. cit.*, p. 135.
[8] The quote is from Norris, "If I Were President," *op. cit.*, p. 2. For specific instances of an attempt to expand civil service in the agencies which he helped to create, see: Norris to Franklin D. Roosevelt, June 7, 1941. Edgar B. Nixon,

The Nebraskan's logic emanated from an understandable emotional rejection of political chicanery and corruption. This emotional response was salutary, but the flaw in his militant urgings of the merit system was that he wanted too much of a good thing. Norris' advocacy of political neutrality had no organizational limits; he made no distinction between persons performing routine clerical and maintenance duties, middle management, and officials responsible for their policy actions to either the President, or Congress, or perhaps both. Norris' concern with the merit system totally ignored the need for politically sensitive and responsive personnel in policy formation and implementation positions.

THE ELECTORAL COLLEGE

Norris criticized the operation of the extra-constitutional party system because he believed it inhibited the popular will, and for the same reason he also criticized the constitutionally sanctioned electoral college. "We will never have the people in control of our Government," he wrote, "until the electoral college is abolished and the voter is given an opportunity to express his choice for the Chief Magistrate of his country." If the states had such an archaic system for the election of governors and lieutenant governors, the people would clamor for a change. The populace submitted to it only because it had always been part of the constitutional framework. Not only was the electoral college "as useless as the fifth

ed., *Franklin D. Roosevelt and Conservation: 1911–1945,* II (Washington, D.C.: Government Printing Office, 1957), 513. Norris maintained that if the Postmaster General would be appointed for a long term, or even dependent on good behavior, then he would be placed far beyond the machinations of partisan politics. All other appointments in the Post Office Department should be made by the Postmaster General from lists compiled by the Civil Service Commission. In 1912 he urged the appointment of a Postmaster General to a ten-year term which would not expire with the President's; in this way he believed the Post Office would be divorced from politics. And in 1935, distressed and upset by President Roosevelt's appointment of James A. Farley, former chairman of the Democratic National Committee, as Postmaster General, he indignantly introduced an unsuccessful bill which required the Postmaster General to be appointed by the President for a ten-year term subject to Senate approval. *Cong. Record,* 62d Cong., 2d sess. (July 10, 1912), Vol. 48, pt. 9, p. 8872. *New York Times,* February 5, 1935, 4:7. See also George W. Norris, "Merit System in the Post Office," *Senate Document No. 439,* 64th Cong., 1st sess. (Washington, D.C.: Government Printing Office, 1916).

wheel of a wagon," but because of its continued existence, Norris insisted, the two great political parties and their national conventions were more readily dominated by political bosses and special interests.[9]

This aversion to the electoral college was neither original nor unique with Norris. It can be traced back to the Jacksonian movement for more direct democracy. Direct election (and a single term for the President and Vice-President) were popular political ideas from 1820 to 1830. In 1922, Norris, imitating a resolution introduced nearly a century earlier by Senator Thomas Hart Benton of Missouri, unsuccessfully introduced a constitutional amendment to elect the President and the Vice-President by direct vote. Again in 1934, Norris introduced a resolution for a constitutional amendment to abolish the electoral college. Norris realized, however, that his resolution, similar in intent to his previously unsuccessful amendment, would never pass unless drastically modified. He recognized certain political realities: the less populous states would oppose such an amendment because of the fear that voters in the Northeast would dominate a popular election; the political leadership of the southern states would also oppose it because they would have to extend the suffrage to Negroes if they were to enjoy the influence in a national popular election to which their population entitled them. Accordingly, he compromised and accepted an amendment to his resolution. The result was that the drastically altered proposed amendment, while providing for abolition of the electoral college, still made the presidential election an election by the states, each state having as many votes as the combined number of senators and representatives to which it is entitled. Despite the change, the debilitated amendment was narrowly defeated.[10] Although Senator Norris never succeeded in making any direct changes in the electoral college, he did suc-

[9] The quotes from Norris are as follows: Norris, "Partisanship," *op. cit.*, p. 15. Norris, "If I Were President," *op. cit.*, p. 14. See also George W. Norris, "The Eagle or the Parrot" (unpublished MS, n.d.), p. 3, Norris Papers.

[10] *Cong. Record*, 67th Cong., 2d sess. (January 4, 1922), Vol. 62, pt. 1, p. 749. *New York Times*, November 20, 1922, 16:3. George W. Norris, "Abolition of the Electoral College," *United States Law Review*, LXVIII (June 1934), 289. For a comprehensive discussion of the problems of altering the method of presidential and vice-presidential selection, see Lucius Wilmerding, Jr., *The Electoral College* (New Brunswick: Rutgers University Press, 1958).

ceed in incorporating in the Twentieth Amendment a minor operational improvement in the electoral mechanism. It is theoretically possible, though extremely unlikely, that when a President is to be chosen in the House of Representatives and a Vice-President in the Senate, a deadlock might occur in both bodies leaving the country without a President or Vice-President on the date of inauguration. In such an untoward occurrence, under the Twentieth Amendment, Congress is given the authority to provide for such contingencies.

While the electoral college system of electing the President and Vice-President needs reform, it is not necessarily for the reasons of more direct democracy and the debilitation of the party structure set forth by Norris. The basic criticism levied against the electoral college is that it may not fairly represent the popular majority. Senator Norris, nonetheless, performed a notable service in bringing to the attention of the American public a serious defect in the American constitutional scheme.

THE LAME DUCK AMENDMENT

Although Norris did not succeed in eliminating the electoral college, he was primarily responsible for the passage of the Twentieth Amendment to the Constitution. Prior to the ratification of the Twentieth, or Lame Duck Amendment, members of Congress were elected in November, and unless a special session of Congress was called by the President, they would not begin their actual service until thirteen months after they were elected to office (eleven months before the next congressional election). Although some incumbents may have failed of re-election, they nevertheless convened with Congress in December and continued to serve throughout the short session until the following March 4. Those members who served the four months after their defeat were dubbed "lame ducks."

Norris recognized that when the Constitution was originally adopted there had been some reason for the long interval between election and the actual commencement of the new Congress. But this practice was no longer valid. "Under a democratic form of government," he correctly insisted, "the wishes of the people should be crystallized into law as soon as possible after those wishes have become known." There was no justification in permitting defeated congressmen to continue legislating. Under such conditions, "a Congress repudiated at the general election may put on the statute books laws that were actually condemned in the preceding election." [11] This situation was also unfair to the legislator. A representative did not begin his work until it was almost time for him to run for renomination and re-election. Consequently, he had a limited legislative record. With longer sessions he would have an adequate record to submit to his constituents.

Another danger of Lame Duck Sessions, the Nebraskan reasoned, was that some lame duck congressmen were particularly susceptible to improper influence. "It has often been true in the past" Norris noted, "that some members of Congress, defeated for re-election, have, during the short session, been absolutely subservient to the wishes of the President in their official capacities, and have willingly obeyed the wishes and commands of political bosses, who are powerful in party machines and in the distribution of Federal patronage." The defeated congressmen, already beyond the censure of the people, would be willing to follow the dictates of the party leaders, knowing that "the man in the White House will be able to compensate him by giving him a better office than the one the people took away from him." [12]

A third danger of short sessions was that legislation considered during this time was subject to the twin and opposing evils of being either too hastily considered or unduly delayed by a filibuster. Frequently important bills could not be studied adequately; the result was what Norris termed "half-baked legislation, with jokers of all kinds getting into the laws." It was impossible, because of the limited time, for the legislators to make themselves fully conversant with matters pending before the Chamber. Furthermore, it often happened that good legislation was killed. Norris maintained that the short session was always fertile ground for filibusters, which, although justified in certain extraordinary circumstances (for example, the Armed Ship bill), were harmful

[11] George W. Norris, "Statement Concerning the Lame Duck" (unpublished MS, January 20, 1933), p. 2, Norris Papers.
[12] George W. Norris, "Coddling the Lame Duck," *The Independent*, CXIV (February 21, 1925), 214. George W. Norris, "Statement" (unpublished MS, n.d.), p. 2, Norris Papers.

because they "take up the time of the Senate and make it practically impossible for it to function as a legislative body." [13]

A final danger was that a Lame Duck Session could defeat democratic political representation. "If it should happen that in the general election in November in presidential years no candidate for President had received a majority of all the electoral votes, the election of a President would then be thrown into the House of Representatives and the membership of that House of Representatives called upon to elect a President would be the old Congress and not the new one just elected by the people." [14]

Nonetheless, despite these compelling reasons for a change in the Constitution, the passage of the Lame Duck Amendment had a tortuous history. On December 5, 1922, Senator Norris introduced his first report supporting his amendment; three times the amendment passed the Senate, but it was not adopted until January 23, 1933, when a sufficient number of state legislatures had voted ratification to make the amendment effective.[15]

The Twentieth Amendment accomplished most of the things Norris hoped it would. It eliminated Lame Duck Sessions; all terms were to end on January 3, at which time Congress would regularly convene. It moved the President's inauguration from March 4 to January 20, thus making both sessions of Congress of indefinite length. And it empowered Congress to provide for choosing a President and Vice-President should something happen to prevent those elected in November of an election year from being inaugurated on the following January 20.

In short, the Twentieth Amendment fulfilled Norris' desire to make Congress more representative of the people's will and removed an illogical situation in which defeated congressmen continued to vote on current policy. But his argument, now moot, that

[13] Norris, "If I Were President," *op. cit.*, p. 6. Norris, "Statement Concerning the Lame Duck," *op. cit.*, p. 3. Norris maintained that his filibuster against the Armed Ship bill was justified because of the transcendent moral issue of America's probable engagement in a European war.

[14] George W. Norris, "Fixing the Commencement of Terms of President, Vice-President, and Members of Congress," *Senate Report No. 170, 68th Cong., 1st sess.* (Washington, D.C.: Government Printing Office, February 22, 1924), p. 4.

[15] For an account of the legislative history of the Twentieth Amendment, see Charles A. Madison, *Leaders and Liberals in Twentieth Century America* (New York: Frederick Ungar Publishing Co., 1961), pp. 344–45.

lame ducks voted the way they did in order to remain in the good graces of the party and the executive so as to receive jobs is open to conjecture. And his contention that the Lame Duck Amendment would substantially curtail filibustering has not been borne out by subsequent legislative history.[16]

The Twentieth Amendment, nonetheless, is an exceedingly important legislative advance with which George W. Norris must be credited. The Lame Duck Amendment and the establishment of the unicameral legislature in Nebraska are his two most significant and lasting contributions to institutionalized legislative reform in the American political system.

THE UNICAMERAL LEGISLATURE

Although George W. Norris is considered the father of the Nebraska unicameral legislature, the only extant single-chamber legislature in the United States, unicameralism has its intellectual antecedents in the progressive movement. The modern movement for the establishment of single-chamber legislatures began in 1912 in Ohio and Oregon and soon spread throughout the country. Nebraska, however, was the only state in which unicameralism took root.[17]

The unicameral movement in Nebraska may be traced to a 1913 joint legislative committee which, after extensive investigation, recommended the abandonment of bicameralism to the 1915 legislative session. The committee unsuccessfully urged the adoption of a constitutional amendment, to be proposed by the initiative, which would establish a unicameral legislature. Throughout the twenties agitation for a unicameral legislature continued, and in 1923 Senator Norris joined the movement. It was not, however, until the general election of 1934, through the constitutional initiative and referendum, that the voters of Nebraska adopted the unicameral legislature.

[16] Franklin L. Burdette, *Filibustering in the Senate* (Princeton: Princeton University Press, 1940), p. 227.

[17] Georgia, Pennsylvania, and Vermont, early in their history, for very brief periods, had a form of unicameral legislature which in actual functioning was a bicameral legislature. John P. Senning, *The One-House Legislature* (New York: McGraw-Hill Book Co., Inc., 1937), p. 75. Alvin W. Johnson, *The Unicameral Legislature* (Minneapolis: University of Minnesota Press, 1938), p. 95. Senning (pp. 39–50) gives an excellent chronological summary of the unicameral movement in the various states.

When Senator Norris came to Lincoln, Nebraska, on February 22, 1934, to commence his active campaign for the unicameral legislature, he delivered an address entitled "The Model Legislature." He began by acknowledging that in establishing new state institutions the early constitutionalists divided the legislative authority between two houses on the theory that "one branch of the legislature would check the other." But the people had now achieved political maturity so that this check was no longer necessary.

For Norris the bicameral legislature was actually a tricameral body because "the conference committee, in reality, comprises a third house." The members of this undemocratic conference committee constituted the most important branch of the legislature. They met in secret and kept no record. In practice, instead of legislation by either the House or the Senate, there was legislation by five or six men who were especially susceptible to the blandishments of lobbyists. In the conference committee "jokers frequently crept into" the laws and the "good things were often taken out." It was only in theory that this legislative excrescence could be democratized. A one-house legislature would make the existence of the conference committee unnecessary.[18]

Somewhat simplisticly, Norris liked to compare the legislature of a state to a great industrial corporation. "The governor is the president of the corporation, the legislature is the board of directors, and the people are the stockholders." The stockholders have a right to know how well the board of directors is representing them, but "with the complexity that comes from a two-house legislature, it is impossible for them to know this." Unicameralism would obviate the large amount of time spent by the voters in following the intricacies of the parliamentary situation, and also make "it impossible for any member of the legislature to shift responsibility or to cover up his vote." The public, thus, could easily ascertain where the legislator stood on all the issues and act accordingly.[19] Only the politicians and the representatives of

[18] George W. Norris, "A Model State Legislature," *New York Times Magazine*, January 28, 1923, p. 12.
[19] The quotes are from a letter by Norris to Kenneth S. Wherry in which Norris developed the logic of the corporation analogy to an absurd extent. Norris to Kenneth S. Wherry, December 12, 1931, Norris Papers. See also: George W. Norris, "The One-House Legislature," *The Annals of the American Academy of Political and Social Science*, CLXXXVI (September 1935), 50–58. George W. Norris, "The One-House Legislature," *National Municipal Review*, XXIV (February 1935), 87–89.

combinations and special interests benefited from the dual-house system. Corruption would be reduced, if not eliminated entirely, and efficiency and integrity take its place. And finally, in a unicameral legislature it would be easier to have nonpartisan representation. Norris could not see why the issues which divide the political parties should in any way be permitted to intrude into state politics. Unicameralism was equated with nonpartisanism and all its virtues.

This was an area in which the Senator was absolutely dogmatic. To Oswald Garrison Villard he wrote that unicameralism "can have only one side; no honest student of government can study the question without coming to the same conclusion." He urged the extension of unicameralism to other states and constantly asserted its merits. Shortly before he died, he stated that he was "more enthusiastically in favor of the unicameral legislature" than he had ever been before.[20]

The Nebraskan was never able to discover any logical argument in favor of a bicameral legislature. He dismissed the claims that bicameralism prevented hasty and careless legislation; that it provided a critical review of legislation passed by the lower house; and that each house remedied the defects in legislation passed by the other. Some of the reasons advanced for the bicameral legislature, he insisted, were the very reasons why bicameralism should be abandoned. The argument that a bicameral legislature was a security against the intrigues of scheming politicians and special interest lobbies had proved to be false. If anything, he asserted, bicameralism sheltered the politician and the lobby. He rejected the contention that a second chamber served as a check against popular passions and impulses; to Norris, the second chamber thwarted the very wishes of the electorate.

It is generally conceded that the Senator's advocacy of the unicameral amendment was the greatest single factor weighing in favor of its passage. Norris' Lame Duck Amendment had just been ratified by the states, and he enjoyed a reputation as a legislative expert as well as an outstanding liberal. However, it should not be forgotten that the unicameral amendment shared the ballot with two other amendments which were exceedingly popular.

[20] Norris to Oswald Garrison Villard, cited in Oswald Garrison Villard, "Pillars of Government: George W. Norris," *The Forum*, XCV (April 1936), 252. Norris to George Handy, March 11, 1944, Norris Papers.

One of them, to repeal Prohibition, was adopted by nearly a 110,000 majority — as compared to a 93,000 majority for the unicameral amendment; the other amendment, authorizing pari-mutuel betting, won by 64,000. In addition, the 1933 Nebraska legislative session had been an inordinately disappointing one, and arguments of efficiency and economy impressed the beleaguered Depression-conscious voter.[21]

In actual practice unicameralism in Nebraska has not proved to be as much of a political panacea as Norris and its proponents had hoped; neither has it proved to be a dismal failure. Adam C. Breckenridge's perceptive evaluation of Nebraskan unicameralism indicates that despite the change in the structure of the legislature "there continues to be a lot of old fashioned lobbying." [22] Although the formal institutional structure may be altered, the basic pressures which operate within the political system remain. In this instance, Norris' belief that a remodeled chamber would alter the operation of the political process has not been borne out. Nonetheless, the establishment of a single-house legislature in Nebraska has brought about some improvements in the legislative process.

The most significant appears to be a procedural improvement. Bills are given greater consideration than formerly, the quantity of bills seems to be reduced, and there is also a "reduction in the number of joker bills and," notes Breckenridge, "the perennials which are the favorite of some constituents and done as a favor." The Senator seems to have been correct in his belief that the elimination of the conference committee would hasten legislation. Furthermore, the unicameral legislature has clearly effected some savings — perhaps insignificant in relation to the total cost of the state government — but nonetheless recurring. There has been a net savings of $35,000 in members' salaries and $8,000 to $10,000 in general legislative expenses a biennium.[23]

The "Nebraska experiment" is no longer an experiment. In their political life, Nebraskans have accepted the single-chamber legis-

[21] Senning, *op. cit.*, pp. 43, 51. Adam C. Breckenridge, *One House for Two: Nebraska's Unicameral Legislature* (Washington, D.C.: Public Affairs Press, 1957), p. vi.
[22] Breckenridge, *op. cit.*, p. 39.
[23] *Ibid.*, p. 51. See also: Roger V. Shumate, "The Nebraska Unicameral Legislature," *Western Political Quarterly*, V (September 1952), 504–12. Donald Janson, "The House Nebraska Built," *Harper's Magazine*, CCXXIX (November 1964), 124–30.

lature so completely that the word "unicameral" has become a noun. The *unicameral* — not the *legislature* — convened, or adjourned, or passed a law. Unicameralism in Nebraska has proved to be a workable and responsible device of representative government. It may well become one of the most viable state political institutions yet devised to meet the needs of a changing federal system.[24] As a reform political structure perhaps it has not yet lived up to the potential predicted by the Senator. But Norris himself recognized that reform in the political system is slow and arduous.

THE JUDICIARY

During the course of his service in Congress, particularly during his tenure as chairman of the powerful Senate Committee on the Judiciary, Norris devoted much thought to what he believed were necessary reforms in the legal system. At one time or another, the Senator manifested an interest in the enactment of uniform laws on the subject of marriage and divorce, the problem of a husband and wife testifying against each other, the procedure and structure of the administrative courts, the adequacy of federal bankruptcy courts, and the operation of criminal procedure in the courts. Furthermore, he constantly, but always futilely, pressured for change in the areas of jurisdiction between federal and state courts.[25]

[24] Since the 1964 Supreme Court holding that apportionment in the states must be on a one person, one vote basis, with each house substantially equal in population. Nebraska's unicameral legislature has received renewed attention. *New York Times,* July 18, 1964, 50:1.

[25] For an elaboration of Norris' views on the issues mentioned, see: *Cong. Record,* 62d Cong., 1st sess. (August 22, 1911), Vol. 47, pt. 5, pp. 4382–83. *Ibid.,* 70th Cong., 2d sess. (January 3, 1929), Vol. 70, pt. 1, pp. 1030–32. Norris to E. V. Morgan, February 29, 1936, Norris Papers. One of Norris' favorite proposals for judicial reform was his suggestion for the abolition of all federal district and circuit courts below the Supreme Court. He wanted to place their jurisdiction in state courts with the right of appeal from state supreme courts to the United States Supreme Court. This proposal, and his allied attempts to limit federal district court jurisdiction, stemmed from his belief that federal judges were too prone to issue antilabor injunctions, and, in general, were pro-business. However, the Norris-LaGuardia Act and subsequent labor legislation have eliminated most of the injunction problems and the 1938 Supreme Court ruling in *Erie Railroad Company v. Tompkins,* which forced federal courts to apply state law, eliminated what Norris considered to be federal arbitrariness. While problems still remain, Norris'

It was not until the Supreme Court began to invalidate New Deal legislation, however, that Norris considered the total political impact of the federal judiciary. After the First Agricultural Adjustment Act was declared unconstitutional (*United States v. Butler,* 1936), in high dudgeon he excoriated the Court for "becoming a continuous constitutional convention." "The people can change the Congress but only God can change the Supreme Court." "An act passed by Congress," he orated wrathfully in the Senate, "should not be declared unconstitutional unless it is unconstitutional beyond a reasonable doubt." And certainly split decisions, particularly five to four decisions, indicated that the Court's nullification of an act was not beyond a reasonable doubt.[26]

Senatorial denunciations notwithstanding, it was continued Court nullification of New Deal measures and FDR's overwhelming re-election in 1936 that brought the problem of an unresponsive Supreme Court into the center of national controversy. In addition to invalidating the AAA, the Court had also declared unconstitutional the NRA, the Guffey Coal Conservation Act, a New York State minimum wage law, and created havoc in the field of labor legislation. At the first congressional session after the election, Senate Majority Leader Joseph T. Robinson and Speaker of the House William B. Bankhead recommended the passage of a constitutional amendment to curb the power of the Court. FDR rejected the idea of amending the Constitution, however, and instead sought a less complicated formula which stressed the diversionary issue of judicial reform. Accordingly, Attorney General Homer Cummings drew up a plan ironically based upon a variation of a 1913 recommendation of Justice McReynolds, now the very epit-

fundamental objections to the federal courts have been largely satisfied. Although Norris was a lawyer, his criticisms of the federal judiciary stemmed not so much from a profound understanding or appreciation of the character and specifics of the American legal system, as from his social and economic beliefs. Perhaps unfairly, he associated the federal judiciary with social and economic reaction. See: George W. Norris, "Criminal Procedures in Our Courts" (unpublished MS, June 24, 1928), p. 1, Norris Papers. George W. Norris, "Abolish Federal Courts?" *New York Times Magazine,* April 23, 1922, p. 5. George W. Norris, "Limiting the Jurisdiction of District Courts of the United States," *Senate Report No. 626,* 70th Cong., 1st sess. (Washington, D.C.: Government Printing Office, March 27, 1928), p. 3. Norris to James E. Lawrence, December 15, 1931, Norris Papers.

[26] *Cong. Record,* 74th Cong., 2d sess. (February 12, 1936), Vol. 80, pt. 2, p. 1883.

ome of judicial recalcitrance, which attempted to create a more liberal atmosphere by enlarging the Court.[27]

The plan called for the President to appoint a new judge for every federal judge with ten years service who remained on the bench six months after reaching the age of seventy. The Supreme Court, however, was not to exceed fifteen and not more than fifty new judges would be added to the lower courts. A hostile reaction from both liberals and conservatives was immediate. Many liberals, Norris included, were queasy about FDR's expedient; they disliked the blatant Court packing and feared the failure to limit the Court's power of review. Some of the liberals, agreeing with FDR on goals but not methods, offered counter proposals. Of these, the plans sponsored by Senators Burton K. Wheeler, William E. Borah, and Norris attracted the most attention. Wheeler advocated a form of recall of judicial decisions by Congress, by a two-thirds vote, after an intervening election. Borah proposed a revision of the Fourteenth Amendment which would allow the states all the powers over social legislation which the Court denied the federal government. And Norris proposed a simple two-part reform. First, Congress would pass a law requiring a two-thirds vote by the Supreme Court to invalidate acts of Congress. Second, a constitutional amendment would establish a nine-year term for the entire federal judiciary, including members of the Supreme Court. In justifying his proposal the Nebraskan reiterated and enlarged the views he had expressed a year earlier in commenting on the AAA decision.

Norris argued that the Constitution divided the power of the government into three equal and coordinate branches: the legislative, the executive, and the judiciary. Each branch should remain within its own sphere to avoid conflict, disorder, and confusion. Although the historical and constitutional antecedents of judicial review were open to academic controversy, Norris averred, it was "fairly well established and settled that at the present time our courts have the right to nullify acts of Congress." [28] Only those

[27] Joseph Alsop and Turner Catledge, *The 168 Days* (New York: Doubleday, Doran and Company, 1938), pp. 18–19. William E. Leuchtenburg, *Franklin D. Roosevelt and the New Deal, 1932–1940* (New York: Harper and Row, 1963), pp. 231–33.

[28] *Cong. Record*, 75th Cong., 1st sess. (March 12, 1937), Vol. 81, pt. 2, p. 2139.

decisions where the Court concurred by a two-thirds majority in declaring legislation unconstitutional would be consonant with tripartite government.

The suggestion that the federal judges occupy their offices for a definite term, rather than for good behavior, was beneficial because judges, once "given unlimited power for life, with luxurious salary, without being responsible to anybody for the use of . . . power, would have a tendency to draw away from the struggles of ordinary humanity." In his desire to make the courts responsive to "ordinary humanity" Norris perhaps neglected to attach sufficient importance to the fact that an independent judiciary could only be attained by permitting judges to enjoy long terms of office, or even life tenure.[29]

Nonetheless, the Norris plan and others were voted down in the Judiciary Committee. The Administration bill was reported out, but with a negative recommendation. Aware that his Court plan had no chance, Norris, in spite of his previous hostility, announced his support of the President's bill.

There is a great outcry against "packing" the Court. But the Court in many recent decisions had been packed, in effect, against the common man, against the people, against the nation trying to save its life. Monopoly, special privilege, the interests of predatory selfishness have lost their old commanding influence at the White House and the Capitol. They are making their last stand in the federal courts. There too often they still have their way. Until these courts are humanized, until in their decisions human rights count equally with property rights, the governmental machinery of democracy is stalled in bringing the country back to life.[30]

But Norris had joined a lost cause. Despite all of FDR's political acumen, the attempt to enlarge the Court failed. It was impossible to break with convention and myth surrounding the Court. The Supreme Court, however, had not always enjoyed such an elevated position of sanctity. Norris' support of legislation designed to smash a judicial blockade was in keeping with the recurring proposal that uninhibited judicial supremacy be curtailed. In 1868, a bill had passed the House which would have required a two-thirds vote

[29] Norris to William A. White, February 22, 1937, Norris Papers. *New York Times*, February 12, 1937, 1:3. *Ibid.*, March 16, 1937, 1:2.
[30] L. H. Robbins, "Norris Restates a Liberal's Credo," *New York Times Magazine*, May 30, 1937, p. 3.

of the Court in order to sustain a decision of legislative unconstitutionality. And of more relevance to Norris' intellectual conditioning was the fact that the Progressive party in 1912 had advocated the recall of judicial decisions, and Robert M. La Follette in his 1924 bid for the presidency had proposed an amendment authorizing Congress to re-enact a law declared unconstitutional by the Supreme Court.[31]

Senator Norris' advocacy of reform in the political process was predicated on his desire to make the institutions of American democracy responsive to the will of the people. Like the Jeffersonians and Jacksonians before him, he and his fellow progressives had an abiding faith in the intelligence and virtue of the American people. Whatever flaws the democratic process possessed could be redressed by more democracy. In spite of Norris' ofttimes unsophisticated explanations for complicated political and social phenomena, he fought in the best tradition of the American progressive spirit. Not only was he aware of the political implications of democracy, but, equally important, he realized that democracy has ethical and economic dimensions.

[31] C. Herman Pritchett, *The American Constitution* (New York: McGraw-Hill Book Co., Inc., 1959), p. 142.

☆　☆　☆　☆　☆　☆　☆　☆　☆

CHAPTER THREE

Economic Democracy

☆　☆　☆　☆　☆　☆　☆　☆　☆

THE STRUGGLE FOR THE DEMOCRATIC VISION

The crusade for structural political reform, an essential element in the ethos of Populism and progressivism, was integrally related to the reformist demand for economic and social advances. "The powers of government — in other words, of the people," the strident Populist platform of 1892 somewhat tautologically but quite unequivocally proclaimed, "should be expanded . . . to the end that oppression, injustice, and poverty shall eventually cease in the land." This ethical touchstone, unattained even today, was still more remote in the "Gay Nineties" — the "gay" decade of widespread agrarian distress, catastrophic labor unrest emphasized by the bloody Homestead and Pullman strikes, the pitiful march of Coxey's Army of unemployed, and a major depression — when the contention between the philosophies of laissez-faire and the interventionist state was growing acute.

This contest, fought in large measure by the Populists and the progressives, has now been settled. It is accepted today — certainly in broad philosophic terms — that the affirmative state may legitimately restrain harsh and unbridled capitalism. The struggle is now over the extent and scope, rarely the very legitimacy, of governmental regulation and intervention. But for George W. Norris, who had matured during the unrestrained exploitation of the Great Barbecue and the ugly tarnish of the Gilded Age, the struggle to establish and expand the affirmative state with its potential promise of economic democracy was a battle still to be fought. Economic individualism, long the prevailing ethic of the American economic order, in the post–Civil War era had grafted on to its classical economic rationale new scientific and religious arguments — the ingenious but sterile philosophies of Social Darwinism and the Gospel of Wealth.

William Graham Sumner and other Social Darwinists, applying to political society Charles Darwin's biological principle of the survival of the fittest, sanctioned the unrestricted right to own and control property as being essential to the selective process. The Gospel of Wealth, in addition, provided a religious justification for economic piracy. This doctrine had a long, if not honorable, intellectual tradition in Calvinist and Puritan thought which stressed the moral righteousness of accumulating wealth through the virtues of industry and frugality. Somewhat less callous than the deterministic approach of the Social Darwinists, the philosophy of the stewardship of wealth projected a shining picture of an American society in which enlightened riches would serve the community. This conception was popularized by evangelist Russell H. Conwell in his incessantly repeated "Acres of Diamonds" lecture and was given a more polished representation by Andrew Carnegie, the millionaire steelmaster, who epitomized its basic premises that private property was the foundation of society, that unrestricted individualism was the proper mode of economic life, and that wealth was the reward of enterprise.

Yet despite the munificence of Carnegie in his endowments of libraries and philanthropies, and the largess of John D. Rockefeller, Leland Stanford, and James B. Duke in their support of universities, doubts arose about the premises of Social Darwinism and the Gospel of Wealth. The doubters, Norris among them, preferred some of the principles of the Social Gospel and Christian Socialism which postulated the belief that the state could and should do something for its citizens. The Social Gospel philosophy, as set forth by its foremost advocate, Washington Gladden, rejected Spencerian competitiveness and its allied doctrine of materialism and preached instead the Golden Rule and the Scripture's admonition that every man is his brother's keeper. The Christian Socialists also stressed the ethical basis of government and emphasized that men, as brothers, should cooperate rather than compete, and that all men, not only the wealthy, were in fact stewards of God's property — the earth. Private ownership of public resources, therefore, was immoral.[1]

George William Norris rejected the Social Darwinian "struggle for existence," and "survival of the fittest," and was closer to some of the doctrines of the Social Gospel and Christian Socialism. (Norris, Bryan, La Follette, Theodore Roosevelt, and Woodrow Wilson had all been molded by the same post–Civil War intellectual ferment, but their responses and approaches to the problems of the free competitive order varied significantly.)

Senator Norris adhered to a conception of American democracy which stressed the political, ethical, and economic importance of the individual, a philosophy predicated on immutable, easily apprehendable, and uncomplicated principles. These principles, clearly stated in the Declaration of Independence — the natural rights trinity of "life, liberty, and the pursuit of happiness" — were the only objects of democratic government. (Senator Arthur Capper of Kansas once referred to Norris as "a living, perambulating Declaration of Independence in human form.") Government, for the Nebraskan, was a "religion that does not consider the conditions which exist beyond the grave but confines its consideration to happiness in this life." Democratic government had an obliga-

---

[1] Christian Socialism had a great many varieties, consequently one can find Christian Socialists advocating all extents of public ownership, ranging from government ownership of a small sector of the economy to extensive government ownership. One of Norris' favorite themes was that all men were entitled to enjoy the benefits of nature. For an excellent discussion of the intellectual currents preceding Populism and progressivism, particularly in relation to their impact on midwestern thinking, see Russel B. Nye, *Midwestern Progressive Politics: A Historical Study of Its Origins and Development, 1870–1958* (East Lansing: Michigan State University Press, 1959), pp. 125–69. Also of interest and importance are: Eric F. Goldman, *Rendezvous with Destiny: A History of Modern American Reform* (New York: Vintage Books, 1956), pp. 66–82. Richard Hofstadter's three books, *The Age of Reform: From Bryan to F.D.R.* (New York: Alfred A. Knopf, 1956); *The American Political Tradition* (New York: Vintage Books, 1954); *Social Darwinism in American Thought* (rev. ed.; Boston: Beacon Press, 1955). Morton White, *Social Thought in America: The Revolt Against Formalism* (Boston: Beacon Press, 1957).

tion to create for its citizens the conditions necessary to the good life. In an article entitled "What Democracy Means to Me," Norris epitomized his vision of the American Promised Land and stressed the need for certain minimal standards of material and psychological well-being:

The government which is the most successful is the government which gives to its people the greatest amount of contentment and happiness. Such a government means a government of homeowners; it means that farms shall be tilled by men who can own the land; and it means that they shall have a recompense, fair and honest, to pay them for their toil, while they are producing the food we eat and the clothing we wear. It means that the laborer must receive a fair compensation for the products produced by the sweat of his face, and in addition he must be able to lay by enough to care for him in comfort and peace in his old age. It means that property must be satisfied with a smaller percentage of the product. It means that those who labor must have more leisure time, they must be better educated; they must spend more time at their firesides. . . .

Unfortunately, however, this democratic vision had to contend with "the intrenched power of wealth and partisan political combination." "Those who bore the advancing torches of light and wisdom would be impeded in their progress and often defeated in their efforts by the powers of intrenched greed, sustained and cemented by those who were opposed to progressive change." The Senator insisted that

the progress of humanity from barbarism to civilization has been one of continuous controversy. Improvements in government have always been bitterly opposed. . . . Every step in the advancement this old world has ever made has been made after a contest. . . . The leaders in every contest toward higher civilization have had to blaze their way through an unknown wilderness, sometimes of doubt and uncertainty, and in this great battle for the rights of the common man and for the further up-building of humanity opposition will be met at every step.

This struggle could be simplified as "a contest between those who wanted to progress and those who did not want to progress . . . between the reactionary and the progressive." [2]

[2] The content of this section has been expressed by Norris in so many of his articles and public addresses that only direct quotations are being cited. His basic premise that a democratic society has a government designed to promote human happiness is the keystone of all his thinking. The quotations, as they appear in the above paragraphs, are all from George W. Norris: "Address at

Perhaps unconsciously, Norris had absorbed some of the ideas of Social Darwinism, but his application of the thesis of an evolutionary struggle to the capitalist economic base assumed definite moral overtones. Norris astutely realized that political democracy is impossible without economic democracy, and that the only way to achieve and insure both was to champion the affirmative state.

DEMOCRATIC TAXATION

The formulation and development of Senator Norris' conception of the affirmative state, with the exception of his views on taxation which reached fruition during the Wilson administration, paralleled and complemented the growth of his political independence. For Norris, misused wealth was always deserving of condemnation and correction, and excessive wealth, in any form, posed a problem for democratic government. To preserve and insure the viability of American democracy it was necessary that judicious federal taxes be imposed. Taxes, essentially a device for the redistribution of wealth, meant "the taking of money from the estates of the very wealthy, where it can perform no real service for humanity, and the giving of it, in the form of taxes, to all the people, from whom it was originally taken, and under whose laws it was accumulated." [3]

As a representative Norris had advocated a graduated inheritance tax but he did not elaborate his views on the subject until, as a freshman senator, on September 8, 1913, he introduced an income tax amendment designed "to break up the very large fortunes." His rationale for this later defeated amendment was essentially an appeal to social consciousness based on a crude

Lincoln Monument Unveiling at Freeport, Illinois, August 27, 1929," reprinted in U.S., *Congressional Record,* 71st Cong., 1st sess. (September 9, 1929), Vol. 71, pt. 3, p. 3421. "What Democracy Means to Me," *Scholastic,* XXXII (May 28, 1938), 29. "Address at the University of Illinois on Receiving the Cardinal Newman Award," November 16, 1933," reprinted in *Cong. Record,* 73d Cong., 2d sess. (January 12, 1934), Vol. 78, pt. 1, p. 523. "Redistribution of Wealth," *Vital Speeches of the Day,* I (February 25, 1932), 330. "Partisanship" (unpublished MS, October 17, 1932), p. 4, Norris Papers. *Cong. Record,* 69th Cong., 1st sess. (June 20, 1926), Vol. 67, pt. 11, p. 11652. For Capper's comment on Norris see Charles A. Madison, *Leaders and Liberals in Twentieth Century America* (New York: Frederick Ungar Publishing Co., Inc., 1961), p. 360.

[3] Norris, "Redistribution of Wealth," *op. cit.,* p. 327.

mixture of Andrew Carnegie's Gospel of Wealth moralizing and Henry George's unearned increment economics popularized in *Progress and Poverty*. He quoted from Andrew Carnegie who, in a mood of self-abnegation, had declared in a famous article in the June 1889 *North American Review* that "by taxing the estates heavily at death the state marks the condemnation of the selfish millionaire's unworthy life." But the steelmaster did not believe — as Norris implied — that the millionaire was *ipso facto* immoral; Norris and Carnegie proceeded from different basic premises. Carnegie accepted ruthless competition as the primary law of society and necessary for all social progress, even though it brought into existence wide disparities in wealth. The rich were those who exercised ability and ambition. When these qualities were rewarded economically it became necessary for the wealthy to use their riches for the welfare of society; but government should not be permitted to confiscate large portions of a man's wealth during his lifetime. Norris, in sharp contrast to Carnegie, believed that the millionaire was *ipso facto* immoral and advocated, in addition to an inheritance tax, a graduated income tax. It was axiomatic that one could not "harvest a crop of millionaires without making an army of paupers." Any undue concentration of wealth was unethical and unwise because it would reflect a situation in which "the profits of human labor and toil went in unfair proportions to those who own the wealth and property of the country."[4]

Supplementing his moral arguments in favor of a progressive tax policy, Norris advocated and uncritically accepted Henry George's unearned increment theory. The Senator was fond of citing the fortune of the Astor family in demonstrating that huge estates should be taken away by the government. When tycoon John Jacob Astor (1864–1912) went down on the *Titanic* and left an estate valued at about $90 million it represented a fantastic increase over the value of the original investment. This, Norris maintained, was property made valuable by the public. Every New York City tax-

[4] The Norris quotes are from *Cong. Record*, 63d Cong., 1st sess. (September 8, 1913), Vol. 50, pt. 5, p. 4423. On December 12, 1910, during a discussion of a taxation bill for the District of Columbia, Norris had pointed out that an inheritance tax, besides raising revenue, was an excellent method "to prevent the entailing of large fortunes" and introduced an amendment to that bill proposing a graduated inheritance tax. *Cong. Record*, 61st Cong., 3d sess. (December 12, 1910), Vol. 46, pt. 1, p. 218. See also Norris: "Redistribution of Wealth," *op. cit.*, p. 3419. "Cardinal Newman Award," *op. cit.*, p. 522.

payer had contributed to the Astor fortune. "From the man in the street who laid the paving blocks to the master minds that planned the giant skyscrapers which lift their heads up in the clouds," he orotundly declared in the Senate, "every one of them has contributed something to the Astors. Every drop of sweat that ever trickled down over the brow of labor on Manhattan Island for a century has contributed its mite to the Astor fortune." This type of wealth had increased because of the increase in property values. Often the investor had not exercised any particular ingenuity or wisdom; sheer circumstance has made his property valuable. "A proper system of taxation would go a good ways, at least, to prevent accumulation of these fortunes by the increase in the value of property." It was only fair that the unearned increment be returned to society after the investor's death.

A progressive inheritance tax, Norris reasoned simplisticly, said to the heir to a fortune: "You cannot take that property which you did not create; you cannot have that immense fortune unless you give the government, under whose laws that fortune was made, whose people really made it, a proper share of it." The inheritance tax, the Nebraskan maintained, had numerous advantages: It was equitable because it levied its tribute after the owner had enjoyed the property during his life, and the persons from whom the extra income would be taken had not worked for the money. Upon the death of the fortune-holder, his property would be itemized and valued in a court of probate; even the beneficiaries, Norris confidently thought, would be interested in seeing that all the property was reported, scheduled, and valued.[5]

In essence the Senator subscribed to the philosophy that the rights to inherit and bequeath property are not natural rights but are given by law. He frequently quoted the social concept of property so well stated by Thomas Jefferson in his letter to James Madison: "The earth belongs in usufruct to the living; the dead have neither powers nor rights over it. The portion occupied by an individual in society ceases to be his when he himself ceases

[5] The Norris quotes are from *Cong. Record*, 63d Cong., 1st sess. (September 8, 1913), Vol. 50, pt. 5, pp. 4424, 4423, 4426. An interesting example of unearned increment was publicized in September 1962 when a plot in mid-Manhattan bought in 1852 for $1,600 sold 100 years later for $380,000. *New York Times*, September 6, 1962, 33:5.

to be, and reverts to society." The Senator pragmatically asserted that

there is a limit beyond which money can buy neither comfort, luxuries, nor pleasures.

If you are possessed of a hundred million dollars, and I have only one million, there is nothing in this world which will bring you any happiness, contentment or pleasure that you can purchase, which I cannot also purchase, without any hardship, or without any injury to my estate. What, then, is the good of this immense fortune, of this useless wealth? If money can do nothing to increase human contentment or happiness, then it is worthless paper.

A man whose only ambition was to make money and who was oblivious to the poverty around him was an enemy of society. He could enjoy no true happiness himself, for all he bequeathed was an excess of gold which was certain to produce an unhappy heritage. Norris insisted with righteous if pessimistic fervor that the heirs to huge fortunes would shortly dissipate their ill-inherited wealth. Such inherited money, he moralized, would be spent "in lavish living, in debauchery, and in gambling." [6]

Although Senator Norris advocated income and inheritance taxes he never mastered the technical nuances and subtleties of the various forms of taxation. His championship of progressive taxation was an expression of a feeling, never a demonstration of extensive technical knowledge (unlike the technical expertise he so frequently revealed during the prolonged Muscle Shoals controversy). While he distinguished between income and inheritance taxes (although both were predicated on the same rationale), he indiscriminately lumped together estate taxes, legacy taxes, death dues, and succession taxes under the rubric of inheritance taxes. And while he asserted that the unearned increment contributed to the accumulation of large fortunes, he never proposed a confiscatory tax on the unearned increment of land values. He never advocated the imposition of Henry George's single-tax theory, although he accepted George's view that the increase in land value comes about because of social causes. He did not perceive the connection, as did the Fabian Socialists, between the unearned increment of land values and the unearned increment on other forms of wealth, especially corporate stocks.

[6] Norris, "Redistribution of Wealth," *op. cit.*, pp. 327, 328, 330. *Cong. Record*, 63d Cong., 1st sess. (September 8, 1913), Vol. 50, pt. 5, p. 4423.

A high progressive income tax and a heavy inheritance tax were necessary to maintain and preserve a sturdy nation of independent businesses and self-reliant middle-class citizens. Norris' tax philosophy — designed to promote this conception of the democratic vision — with the exception of his suggestion during his last senatorial term that vigorous taxation be used to control rampant inflation, never extended to the more sophisticated level of an instrument of government planning and control; its primary purpose was always equalization. Senator Norris, nevertheless, correctly realized that taxation could not by itself reduce the pronounced inequalities in the economic system and establish an economic order based on the moral concept of equality for economic progress. To achieve a flourishing society, Norris also advocated extensive government regulation, and in some economic areas, government ownership.

REGULATION FOR DEMOCRACY

The conception of a limited mission of the federal government, epitomized by the shibboleth "that government is best which governs least" as a working tenet of the laissez-faire ethic, was seriously questioned after the Civil War. As the agrarian base of the American economy began to decline, modern industry and finance capitalism began to rise. Beginning in the 1870's, the characteristic American individualistic-competitive system began to give way to a corporate system with a high degree of concentration and control. Once the corporation became the major business institution, new business arrangements, notably the trust, began to be predominant in the economy. The trust, an advance over the not too successful pooling agreements which attempted to limit free competition, now effectively limited competition and established prices. Thomas C. Cochran and William Miller have noted that "the Standard Oil Company set the trust pattern in 1879, and so effectively did it operate under this new type of business enterprise that in the next decade appeared the Cottonseed Oil Trust, the Linseed Oil Trust, the Salt Trust, the Lead Trust, the Leather Trust, the Cordage Trust, the Sugar Trust, until by the 1890's the term trust was applied invidiously to every seeming monopoly." As the United States entered the twentieth century the merger movement reached its peak in the years 1898 through 1902, and transformed many industries once composed of many small and medium-sized firms into industries in which one or a very limited number of enterprises dominated.[7]

As the trusts were emerging, the antitrust sentiment, marshaled by western and southern agrarian protest against railroads and monopolies, was gaining momentum. Professor Arthur Link notes that "by 1890 at least fourteen states and territories had written antitrust provisions into their constitutions, while thirteen others had adopted antitrust provisions." [8] Congress, in that year, recognizing — or at least paying lip service to — the necessity of regulating excessive combination and consolidation and of preserving competition, passed the Sherman Antitrust Act. But few antitrust cases were instituted and those that reached the courts only gave encouragement to the merger movement. (In 1895, the Supreme Court ruled that the American Sugar Refining Company's almost complete monopoly was not affected by the Sherman Act; not until 1904 did the Supreme Court order its first dissolution of a monopoly under the 1890 Act.) It was, accordingly, in Norris' first term in the House of Representatives that the first big antitrust crusade was launched by President Theodore Roosevelt.

The Nebraskan enthusiastically endorsed and suggested militant action against the trusts. In January 1905, he introduced an unsuccessful resolution to increase the powers of the Interstate Commerce Commission. That same year he announced his willingness to amend the Constitution because "Congress should have the power to regulate life insurance." It was doubtful if Congress could assume regulation of insurance under either the taxing power or the interstate commerce power, hence a constitutional amendment was necessary. In the House he often spoke indignantly against the oppressive combinations, and in his last year as a representative he delivered, in a manner foreshadowing his later

[7] Sidney Fine, *Laissez Faire and the General Welfare State: A Study of Conflict in American Thought, 1865–1901* (Ann Arbor: University of Michigan Press, 1956), p. 167. Thomas C. Cochran and William Miller, *The Age of Enterprise: A Social History of Industrial America* (rev. ed.; New York: Harper Torchbooks, 1961), p. 142. Ralph L. Nelson, *Merger Movements in American Industry, 1895–1956* (Princeton: Princeton University Press, 1959), pp. 4–5.
[8] Arthur S. Link, *American Epoch: A History of the United States Since the 1890's* (New York: Alfred A. Knopf, 1956), p. 111.

famous "Spider Web of Wall Street" speech, a carefully prepared attack against the coffee trust. Although it was his most ambitious address as a congressman, his colleagues, unimpressed, did not undertake, as Norris had hoped, an investigation of the coffee trust. The immediate result of the speech, aside from a non-productive investigation by a special attorney of the Department of Justice, was not apparent. However, in gathering data Norris clarified some of his views on the control of trusts — an issue to which he devoted considerable attention as a senator.[9]

Norris' first senatorial campaign coincided with the presidential election campaign of 1912, in which all three parties (Republican, Progressive, and Democratic — the Socialists proceeded from different assumptions) advocated strengthened antitrust legislation. Honoring his campaign promises, on January 20, 1914, President Wilson addressed a joint session of Congress and requested antitrust legislation. The President's recommendations were embodied in five bills, but after several weeks of hearings, two major bills emerged: the Trade Commission bill and the Clayton bill.

Freshman Senator Norris righteously concurred in Wilson's indictment of the trusts. The trust directors were more than malefactors of great wealth; they were "in the eyes of humanity and in the eyes of God . . . the worst criminals outside of jail." To successfully solve the trust problem, the Nebraskan maintained that Congress should enact laws that would make one of two things certain: "One of them is that you must provide, by proper criminal law, jail sentences for those who organize and control trusts in violation of law. Another way is to make it financially unprofitable for anybody or any set of men to organize a trust. . . . If you will send a few trust magnates to jail, that will break it up. If you will pass a law that will make it financially unprofitable to organize trusts, that will break it up." However, he always stressed that although Congress had plenary right to regulate corporations, Congress must impose upon itself the moral obligation of effecting regulation "that would not be destructive of the property of a corporation or take its property without due process of law, even

---

[9] *Cong. Record*, 58th Cong., 3d sess. (January 30, 1905), Vol. 39, pt. 2, p. 1618. *Ibid.*, 59th Cong., 1st sess. (December 16, 1905), Vol. 40, pt. 1, p. 509. Richard Lowitt, *George W. Norris: The Making of a Progressive, 1861–1912* (Syracuse: Syracuse University Press, 1963), pp. 213–15.

though we should conceive that it would be for the public good to do it." [10]

During the discussion of the Clayton bill, Norris expressed dismay at the laxity of federal antitrust enforcement and offered an unsuccessful amendment:

. . . The Attorney General of any State, may, at the cost and expense of the State, bring suit in the name of the United States, in any district court of the United States having jurisdiction over the parties to enforce any of the anti-trust laws; Provided: that at least ninety days before commencing suit the Attorney General of the State has requested the Attorney General of the United States to bring such suit and such request has not been complied with by the Attorney General of the United States [who] shall have the right to appeal and participate in said suit with said Attorney General of the State.[11]

The Senator believed that his amendment was very much like state *quo warrante* proceedings, where the state attorney general is first given authority to try the right of a man to hold office, but if he does not take action, any interested state citizen has a right to ask him to commence such an action. Nonetheless, even if the Norris amendment had become part of the Clayton Act, it is doubtful if the trust laws would have been much more vigorously enforced. In most states, at that time, despite political agitation to the contrary, corporate control of the political process was an accomplished fact.

The Nebraskan also supported Senator Lane's amendment which provided that the Secretary of the Treasury, and in cases affecting the War and Navy Departments, the Secretaries of those Departments would be authorized to pay as a reward 10 per cent of any sum which would be recovered in the nature of penalties and fines to whoever first furnished evidence to the government of violations of the antitrust or interstate commerce laws.

When the conference report on the Clayton bill came out, Norris,

[10] *Cong. Record*, 63d Cong., 2d sess. (October 2, 1914), Vol. 51, pt. 16, pp. 16044, 16051. Norris was skeptical about criminal prosecution. "Any man who has had any experience in prosecution, knows that it is very difficult to obtain convictions, and in addition to that, it often occurs that the man who could be convicted would only be a hired man — that the real power and the real wrongdoer would be somewhere in the background." Norris to F. A. Good, June 15, 1914, Norris Papers.
[11] *Cong. Record*, 63d Cong., 2d sess. (September 1, 1914), Vol. 51, pt. 14, p. 14525.

incensed by the deletion of the original criminal penalties, angrily declared that if enacted into law in the form in which it emerged from the conference committee it would "have the appearance of having passed through John D. Rockefeller's Sunday School Class rather than through the Congress of the United States." [12] He preferred to take the responsibility for having defeated the conference report than have the bill passed in its shameful conference committee version. After Wilson signed the Clayton Act, Norris reaffirmed his dislike for the measure, calling it "a makeshift, a delusion, a snare, and a fraud." Senator James A. Reed, agreeing in equally strong language, characterized the newly passed measure as "a sort of legislative apology to the trusts, delivered hat in hand, and accompanied by assurances that no discourtesy is intended." [13] That same session Congress passed the Federal Trade Commission Act which created a Federal Trade Commission charged with enforcing the Clayton Act. In contrast to the sweeping language of the Sherman Act, the Clayton Act specifically prohibited practices which tended to control markets. For example, it condemned price discrimination, exclusive selling or leasing contracts, and certain corporate stock combinations.

Despite his disgust at what he considered toothless legislation, Norris, nonetheless, made a public appeal for the support of the FTC. By exposing and publicizing the nefarious practices of the trusts, the public would benefit. The Nebraskan, therefore, prodded the Federal Trade Commission in the hope that more effective regulation could be achieved. In 1922 he introduced a resolution calling on the FTC to investigate a proposed merger of the Armour-Morris meatpacking companies. In 1923 he introduced a resolution for an FTC investigation of the amount and ownership of the chief kinds of wealth in the United States; in 1926 he offered a resolution to have the FTC report the names and capitalization of corporations that had issued stock dividends, together with the amount of dividends before and after the Supreme Court's ruling that such dividends were not taxable; and in 1929, afraid of the increasing economic strength and expansion of the power companies into other areas of the economy, he requested

[12] *Ibid.*, 63d Cong., 2d sess. (October 2, 1914), Vol. 51, pt. 16, p. 16043.
[13] *Ibid.*, 63d Cong., 3d sess. (February 8, 1913), Vol. 52, pt. 4, p. 3411. Link, *op. cit.*, p. 133.

the FTC to investigate the "nation-wide activity on the part of the Power Trust to buy the newspapers of the country." [14]

Despite these resolutions, by the mid-twenties Senator Norris was urging the abolition of the FTC. He realized that the objectives of the antitrust legislation required not only the enactment of a law, but its enforcement as well. But vigorous antitrust regulation declined after America entered World War I and when the Democratic Wilson administration was followed by successive Republican administrations. Republican appointments to the independent regulatory commissions debilitated the enforcement mechanisms. Captured by its clientele, the FTC, Norris noted, had become "the refuge for monopoly, unfair competition, and unfair business methods." [15] Writing in *The Nation*, Norris perceptively commented that appointments "made ostensibly for the purpose of giving effect to legislative acts of Congress have raised a query in the minds of millions of law-abiding citizens as to whether a studied effort is not under way to put into office executive officials who are not honestly in sympathy with the enforcement of many of our regulatory laws." [16] He was particularly distressed about appointments to the Interstate Commerce Commission, the Federal Trade Commission, and the Attorney Generalship. "The result is that their operations are more or less a farce. Indirectly they give to Big Business the privileges it would have if there were no commission, and in addition to this, such monopolies can say to the country that they have a clean bill of health given to them by this commission, which in practical effect, is the same as though they had been investigated by themselves." [17]

The Senator was unhappy about the appointment of Charles Warren as Attorney General because he felt Warren's business life had been spent in carrying out the activities of the Sugar Trust. "To appoint one of the representatives of this gigantic monopoly," Norris wrote, "as head of the great Department of Justice, whose

---

[14] *New York Times*, December 31, 1922, 21:8. *Ibid.*, February 27, 1923, 21:5. *Ibid.*, December 22, 1926, 3:5. *Cong. Record*, 71st Cong., 1st sess. (May 20, 1929), Vol. 71, pt. 2, p. 1526.

[15] *Ibid.*, 69th Cong., 1st sess. (March 20, 1926), Vol. 67, pt. 6, p. 5966.

[16] George W. Norris, "Boring from Within," *The Nation*, CXXI (September 16, 1925), 297.

[17] George W. Norris, "The Federal Trade Commission" (unpublished MS, November 17, 1925), p. 3, Norris Papers.

duty it is to protect the people from this wrong and to prosecute those who are guilty of violating the antitrust laws, is, in every practical sense, a nullification of these laws, as effective as a repeal by act of Congress." [18] He was equally unhappy about the appointment of Thomas F. Woodlock as a member of the Interstate Commerce Commission. Woodlock, in the Senator's eyes, was a railroad man and thus should, in every moral sense, have been debarred from holding a seat on the ICC, which was created primarily to regulate the railroads.

When former representative William E. Humphrey, an advocate of big business who hoped that the Commission would no longer be used as "a publicity bureau to spread socialist propaganda," was appointed chairman of the Federal Trade Commission, Norris summed up his distress and indignation at the attenuation of the regulatory enforcement by stating:

All of these commissions were established for a definite purpose. They came into existence in answer to an honest demand for the work which the law delegates to them. The anti-trust laws are likewise on the statute books for the purpose of curing admitted evils. Are we now to nullify these laws: Are we to go back to the beginning and permit monopoly to have full sway, without any governmental curb? The effect of these appointments is to set the country back more than twenty-five years. It is an indirect but positive repeal of Congressional enactments, which no Administration, however powerful, would dare to bring about by any direct means. It is the nullification of federal law by a process of boring from within.[19]

At times Norris publicly wondered why, if the trusts, combinations, and big business were to run the country, they should not be permitted to do so directly, rather than through the expensive machinery which was originally established for the protection of the people against monopoly and control. The Federal Trade Commission, he suggested bitterly, should be abolished until such time as there was an executive who had some sympathy with the conception of regulation in the public interest. Not only had the FTC been lax in enforcing the law, but it had compounded its misfeasance by following a set of procedural rules which had all the flavor of a star-chamber proceeding. Under the administration of Humphrey, the FTC rules had been changed so that when com-

[18] Norris, "Boring from Within," *op. cit.*, p. 297.
[19] *Ibid.*

plaints came in, those against whom the charges were made were permitted a secret hearing. And if at that hearing the trust pleaded guilty to violation of the law, it was slapped on the wrist and told not to continue its violation.[20] The government's powerful weapon of "pitiless publicity" had been abandoned.

But this concern over the decline of regulation exhibited by Norris and shared by the La Follette progressives did not extend to most public officials or to the general public. The laxity in enforcing the antitrust legislation was but a reflection of the prevailing approbation which business, particularly big business, enjoyed during the 1920's. Businessmen were now "captains of industry," not the "robber barons" of the Populist unrest or the "malefactors of great wealth" of the Progressive era. Bruce Barton, a leading advertising apostle of the business order, went so far as to picture Jesus in the image of the businessman. It was in this climate that the second large merger movement occurred.

The new wave of consolidation which took place from 1926 through 1930, Nelson writes, "represented attempts to restore the industrial concentration achieved by the first merger wave, a concentration which had become diluted over the years," and to some extent, it reflected the emergence of new leading industries.[21] The 1928 presidential campaign occurred at the midpoint of this merger movement. In the sixteen years that separated the 1928 campaign from the turbulent 1912 electoral contest an intellectual, social, and economic revolution had taken place. Now both major parties, in a nearly complete philosophical somersault, embraced the self-regulating economy. The new Republican President, Herbert Hoover, appropriately the former Secretary of Commerce, had defeated Alfred E. Smith and the Democratic party, whose national chairman, John J. Raskob, was also chairman of General Motors. But public belief and adulation of the unregulated business system collapsed with the stock market on Black Friday, 1929.

Elected in 1932 during the ensuing Great Depression, Franklin Delano Roosevelt, in his electrifying first inaugural message, promised to drive the money-changers from the temple. But the First New Deal, interested more in recovery than in reform did not press

[20] *Cong. Record*, 69th Cong., 1st sess. (March 20, 1926), Vol. 67, pt. 6, p. 5966.
[21] Nelson, *op. cit.*, p. 5.

antitrust action. To the contrary, the National Industrial Recovery Act, presented to Congress on May 15, 1933, which spearheaded the Administration's anti-depression measures, sanctioned industrial self-regulation. Senator Norris was willing "to give up some of our ideas and some of the ideas of our forefathers regarding competition," although he could not fully support the NIRA with its provisions for suspension of the Sherman Act.[22] Only three months before the NIRA was presented to Congress, Norris had delivered his "Spider Web of Wall Street" speech against the tendency toward concentration and control.

As changes in finance capitalism had taken place the Nebraskan had shifted his attack; although after the 1920's he still spoke about the evil machinations of the trusts, he was now chiefly concerned with the proliferation of holding companies. Holding companies had become the greatest evil in the economic system because, like the oldtime trust, they eliminated free competitive forces from the marketplace. The control of all business was rapidly drifting toward corporations which were "compelled, whether they like it or not, to obey the mandate that comes from Wall Street." Norris, in a manner reminiscent of the 1913 Pujo Committee, displayed charts to illustrate that there was a money trust controlled by J. P. Morgan and Company. The United States had reached the point where "the business of the country is controlled by men who can be named on the fingers of one hand, because these men control the money of the nation, and that control is growing at a rapid rate." [23] When money usage is controlled, the banks are controlled, and in turn all other corporate institutions in society become beholden to Wall Street and the financiers. Banks through the device of interlocking directorates could control practically any corporation in the country.

All society was forced to depend upon the largess of behemoths. In view of their pervasive influence on the economy, "holding companies have no excuse for their existence." "In most of the cases the only reason for their existence," Norris stated, "is to deceive the people who pay the money, and to make profits for those who sit at the top of the holding companies, and who sell stocks, made

[22] Norris to Clarence M. Westbrook, June 5, 1933, Norris Papers.
[23] *Cong. Record*, 72d Cong., 2d sess. (February 23, 1933), Vol. 76, pt. 5, p. 4778.

mostly of water in many cases, to the investing public, and thus deceive them as well as the customers who pay the money." The holding company was civilization's greatest enemy.[24]

Some months after the "Spider Web of Wall Street" speech Senator Norris received the Cardinal Newman Award at the University of Illinois. He used the occasion to summarize, in a simple and forthright way, his views:

Every form of government implies certain curtailment of personal liberty. Without such curtailment we could have no government, and as our civilization becomes more complex and as new and heretofore unknown elements enter into the proposition, the personal rights of individuals must give way to the human rights of people generally which are necessary for the perpetuation of any government and any form of society . . . the accumulation of the property or the money of any country in the hands of a comparatively few men is injurious to society, and a drawback upon the progress of humanity. Neither can we close our eyes to the disclosures which have been made from time to time of the unreasonable power wielded by men of great wealth, and the wicked and inhuman way in which these men have tried to control even the policies of our federal government.[25]

For the Nebraskan the ultimate test was that "when any monopoly or combination is able to control economic conditions so as to compel the people to sign away their rights and their liberty of action, then the rights of society must be preserved by legal means in order to restrain the oppression of the powerful over the weak." [26]

The acceptance of some of the logic in Norris' arguments was seen in the actions of the Second New Deal. In the spring of 1938 FDR sent a special message to Congress calling for an extensive study of the concentration of economic power; Professor Thurman Arnold of the Yale Law School reinvigorated the Antitrust Division of the Department of Justice; and the Temporary National Economic Committee began its exhaustive, albeit ultimately ineffective, inquiry into the economy.

Although the social justice principles of the Second New Deal were never completely realized, a pattern in the progressive image had gained new acceptance and renewed viability. In the years

---

[24] *Ibid.*, 72d Cong., 1st sess. (July 13, 1932), Vol. 75, pt. 14, p. 15204.
[25] Norris, "Cardinal Newman Award," *op. cit.*, p. 521.
[26] George W. Norris, "Behind the Political Smokescreen," Radio Address over the Columbia Broadcasting System, June 14, 1936, reprinted in *Cong. Record*, 74th Cong., 2d sess. (June 16, 1936), Vol. 80, pt. 9, p. 9605.

after Norris' death, the concept of effective and sustained government regulation was periodically resuscitated. The Antimerger Act of 1950 was added to legislation existing during Norris' life and new activities brought into the scope of the antitrust laws. The Federal Trade Commission, aware of the inadequacies of regulation, is still trying to unravel the extent of interlocking financial arrangements between large corporations to "form a stronger basis for antitrust enforcement and to provide the agency with a pool of reliable data for use in advising other government agencies and Congress on power concentrations in key industries." [27] Obviously much remains to be achieved. Norris recognized that "in every great struggle, after victory has been attained and a step in progress has been made, it is found that special interests have taken advantage of conditions for their own selfish enrichment, and, while the main object has been accomplished, many new evils have crept into the governmental fabric." [28]

Norris, always an opponent of special interests, belonged to that group of progressives who, in Arthur Mann's words,

were the first to call attention to the unequitable distribution of the national income and to do something about it. They taxed, policed, lectured, and scolded big business so effectively that the power and arrogance of a J. P. Morgan is unthinkable today. They built a number of devices into the economy to cushion the shock of those who falter in the race for life. More so than any other group in America they transformed the social Darwinian jungle of some eighty years ago into the humane capitalistic society it is today.[29]

But Norris went beyond "taxing," "policing," and "scolding" — all areas acceptable today. Norris advocated, in addition, selective and judicious use of government ownership and operation — an extreme position which, to the majority today seems politically unrealistic and pragmatically unnecessary.

DEMOCRATIC OWNERSHIP AND OPERATION

The week after George W. Norris became thirty-one, the People's Party of America met on July 4, 1892, in Omaha, Nebraska, in

[27] *Wall Street Journal*, January 16, 1963, 1:6.
[28] Norris, "Lincoln Monument Address," *op. cit.*, p. 3419.
[29] Arthur Mann, "The Progressive Tradition," *The Reconstruction of American History*, ed. John Higham (New York: Harper and Brothers, 1962), p. 178.

their first national convention. Celebrating the 116th anniversary of the Declaration of Independence, the Populists issued a militant platform which had as one of its central demands (after the free and unlimited coinage of silver and gold at the legal ratio of 16 to 1, the graduated income tax, and the establishment of governmental postal savings banks) a firm statement on government ownership.

We believe that the time has come when the railroad corporations will either own the people or the people must own the railroads. . . . Transportation being a means of exchange and a public necessity, the government should own and operate the railroads in the interest of the people. The telegraph, telephone, like the post-office system, being a necessity for the transmission of news, should be owned and operated by the government in the interest of the people.

In this basic demand the Populists brought to its logical consummation the idea of public regulation of railroads which was an outgrowth of the Granger movement and the farmers' alliances. Since the 1870's the railroads had been a central concern of the agitated midwestern and southern farmers. By the time Norris was elected to his first term as a representative, this agitation had resulted in the adoption by many states (as early as the 1870's, Illinois, Wisconsin, Minnesota, and Iowa had established railroad commissions and attempted to prescribe equitable rates) and the federal government of a policy of ostensible railroad regulation.

The Interstate Commerce Act of 1887, administered by a federal commission, was supposed to police railroad practices but the Supreme Court's narrow interpretation of the Commerce Act emasculated the Interstate Commerce Commission. The issue of federal railroad regulation was resuscitated by the progressives who, to the basic Act of 1887, added the Elkins Act of 1903 which forbade price discriminations and rebates; the Hepburn Act of 1906 which enlarged the ICC and its powers; the Mann-Elkins Act of 1910 which empowered the ICC to suspend general rate increases and to revise rates on its own initiative; the Panama Canal Act of 1912 which strengthened ICC jurisdiction over joint rail and water traffic; and the Physical Valuation Act of 1913 which was to serve as the basis for rate-making by the ICC.

Initially in agreement with the prevalent progressive concept of railroad regulation, Norris ultimately outdistanced progressive concepts and embraced the more radical proposals of government ownership. The Nebraskan's agrarian background had imbedded in him strong views concerning the pivotal importance of railroad transportation. He believed that "among the activities of humanity, transportation . . . is the most important." The price of transportation entered into some part of the cost of everything which one ate or wore. As civilization develops, Norris reasoned, the cost factor of transportation increases in importance. "It is a part of the cost of the cradle in which our childish fears are soothed, of the coffin in which we are laid in the ground, and a material part of the monument which stands at our grave. It is a tax which none can escape." Whoever "controls transportation wields enormous power for good or ill over the lives of his fellow creatures." Norris feared that the railroads might control huge portions of the economy and also become an evil influence on the political process.[30] This

[30] George W. Norris, "Keeping the Railroads Out of Politics" (unpublished MS, n.d.), p. 1, Norris Papers. Walter Locke, "George W. Norris, Independent," *Antioch Review*, V (June 1945), 279. Norris was also interested in the problem of stockyards control, and suggested in the Senate that they be "publically owned, publically controlled, publically managed, the same as any other market place for the benefit of the public without the view of producing profit to anybody." Public ownership of the stockyards was necessary because the meatpacking trust prevented the market from operating according to the laws of supply and demand. If the government owned the actual marketplace, the small livestock producers would have a place to sell their animals free from the pressures of a situation in which the marketplace was owned by the big packers. It was necessary "to have competition in such things as the packing business" because it was "so closely connected with the cost of living." Aware of political realities, Norris recognized that Congress would not approve of government ownership of the stockyards and compromised on federal regulation. In 1921 he suggested that a federal livestock commissioner be established within the Department of Agriculture to prevent a packers' monopoly and the arbitrary raising of prices. This proposal received limited acceptance in the Packers and Stockyards Act of that year, which empowered the Secretary of Agriculture to regulate rates and practices in the handling of livestock and live poultry.

In addition to Senator Norris' sustained interest in public ownership of the transportation and power industries, at various times in his career he manifested an interest in other areas of government ownership. In January 1914, Norris submitted a Senate resolution requesting the Postmaster General to investigate the possibilities of government acquisition of the telegraph and telephone facilities to be operated as an adjunct to the postal service. That same year he suggested that the government manufacture for itself items which it used. Competition with private concerns was justified, he believed, if the government was not receiving fair treatment. He also suggested that the government manufacture its own armor plate because "the government has a right to make articles needed for its own use," and also because "in case of emergency the government will not be dependent on private

attitude had been engendered by the fact that in Nebraska at one time the railroads had had their own free will in making rates as well as in designating governors, legislatures, and congressmen.[31]

To reduce the threat of railroad domination and to protect the consuming public, Norris continually submitted resolutions calling on the Interstate Commerce Commission to conduct investigations into the affairs of the railroads. Not content with this, he also introduced bills designed to tighten public control. Still a freshman senator, in 1914 he introduced a bill to amend the Interstate Commerce law "to make it impossible for a few financial pirates to wreck a railroad." Despite the fact that it was subsequently reintroduced in successive Congresses, this ambitious bill never received senatorial approval.[32]

In essence, the Norris bill made it unlawful for any interstate common carrier to purchase the stock or the corporate property of any other corporation without the prior consent of the Interstate Commerce Commission. The bill also tried to eliminate corruption by making it a penal crime for a carrier's agent to give money or a free pass or bestow other consideration on a public official. The overriding philosophy and justification for this legislation was the Senator's belief that every railroad is a quasi-public institution.[33] During the 1916 controversy over the eight-hour day, Norris sug-

parties for armor plate." Many years later, in 1939 when America was rearming, he urged the government to manufacture its own powder, ships, and airplanes. See: *Cong. Record*, 63rd Cong., 2d sess. (January 12, 1914), Vol. 51, pt. 2, p. 1503. *Ibid.*, 63d Cong., 2d sess. (January 21, 1914), Vol. 51, pt. 2, p. 2038. *Ibid.*, 67th Cong., 1st sess. (June 17, 1921), Vol. 61, pt. 3, p. 2709. Norris to H. L. Williams, January 6, 1924, Norris Papers.

[31] Lowitt, *Making of a Progressive, op. cit.*, pp. 231–32, describes an instance in which Representative Norris succeeded in limiting the Union Pacific Railroad's right of way.

[32] George W. Norris, "Statement: In re Norris Railroad Bill" (unpublished MS, n.d.), Norris Papers. Illustrative of the resolutions Norris offered would be: A resolution requesting the Attorney General to inform the Senate if the various combinations of railroads were in violation of the Sherman Antitrust Act or any other statute and whether the Department of Justice had in contemplation any action for the dissolution of these combinations. *Cong. Record*, 63d Cong., 2d sess. (June 1, 1914), Vol. 51, pt. 10, p. 9507. A resolution requesting the ICC to reopen an investigation into the affairs of the railroads to see if any financial juggling had taken place. *Ibid.*, 63d Cong., 2d sess. (February 6, 1914), Vol. 51, pt. 3, p. 3024.

[33] *Cong. Record*, 64th Cong. 1st sess. (January 25, 1916), Vol. 53, pt. 2, p. 1496. As early as 1908 Norris had touched on the concept that banks were quasi-public institutions. See *ibid.*, 60th Cong., 1st sess. (January 7, 1908), Vol. 42, pt. 1, p. 521.

gested that in the battle between railroad management and railroad labor there was a third party, the public. "We are too apt to forget," he declared in the Senate, "that the public have rights that are at least equal to the rights of any other interested parties." [34]

When, as a war measure in 1917, the government did take over the railroads, Norris, initially pleased, soon became disillusioned. "Those who believe in government operation of the railroads," he complained, "would themselves be the last to advocate the operation of the railroads by a Cabinet officer of any administration or to put them in the hands of any President or any other political force." [35]

After the war, beginning in 1919, the problem of the disposition of the railroads arose. William G. McAdoo, who had resigned as Wilson's Secretary of the Treasury to become director general of the Railroad Administration, recommended a five-year experiment in public operation. Glenn E. Plumb, a lawyer for the railroad brotherhoods, went even further and suggested the nationalization of the railroads with the workers participating in management and receiving a share of the profits. Norris contributed to the ferment by futilely introducing a bill for outright government ownership of the railroads. All these drastic proposals were rejected for the more moderate but nonetheless advanced position of the Esch-Cummins Transportation Act of 1920. The Act, named after two progressive midwestern Republicans, Representative John J. Esch of Wisconsin and Senator Albert B. Cummins of Iowa, provided for some extremely stringent federal control of railroads (the ICC was given rate control and supervision over the sale of railroad securities). But the Act also recognized the need for carrier stability and so authorized mergers and traffic pooling with the approval of the ICC. But as alternate forms of transportation — highway, water, and air — grew increasingly competitive, the Act of 1920 became ill-adapted to the technological and economic dynamics of the transportation revolution.

In 1924 Senator Norris submitted a bill which represented the culmination of his legislative thought on the question of railroad control. When he had started his study of the transportation question he was "bitterly opposed to government ownership," but he had finally come to the conclusion that it was necessary because

[34] *Ibid.*, 64th Cong., 1st sess. (September 2, 1916), Vol. 53, pt. 13, p. 13635.
[35] *Ibid.*, 66th Cong., 2d sess. (December 4, 1919), Vol. 59, pt. 1, pp. 123–24.

"private ownership and operation, combined with government regulation, has been an expensive failure, and whether we wish it or not, the logic of events has driven us to the only remedy remaining, government ownership and operation." [36]

The Norris transportation bill of 1924, utilizing a government corporation, was designed to regulate interstate commerce and provide transportation at cost. Not only could it construct railroads anywhere in the United States, it could also purchase any railroad by condemnation proceedings or at private sale (provided that the amount paid should not exceed the valuation placed upon the railroad by the Interstate Commerce Commission). Furthermore, the bill provided that the government should turn over to the corporation its merchant ships and all its boats and barges in use on the inland rivers. (The objective was to regulate transportation charges all over the country.) The corporation, going beyond the carriage aspect of transportation, was also empowered to construct dams for the purpose of generating electricity to be used for power and likewise to acquire and operate coal mines for the same purpose. Financing was to be arranged by having the Secretary of the Treasury issue United States bonds, drawing interest not to exceed 4½ per cent.

According to a Norris press release, "about the only thing the government does in the operation besides giving the corporation the right to build dams upon the public streams and right of way through public lands, and turning over its unused ships, is to lend to this corporation its credit. There will be no profit, there will be no dividends, there will be no stock, and hence nobody to get any profit out of the operation. It will be transportation at absolute cost." [37]

The requirement of government ownership of all water transportation was thoroughly consistent with the Senator's previously

[36] *New York Times*, January 15, 1924, 28:1. Norris to James A. Reed, January 22, 1931, Norris Papers. George W. Norris, "If I Were President" (unpublished MS, n.d.), p. 22, Norris Papers. This same sentiment, in somewhat more pithy language, was reiterated some years later by Norris in a letter to a constituent. "I have about reached the conclusion that the only remedy is government ownership and operation of the railroads. We have had regulation for a great many years both in the Nation and in the State as to railroads and other public utilities, but this regulation has not been successful." Norris to Victor Bal, February 27, 1931, Norris Papers.
[37] George W. Norris, "Statement: In re Norris Railroad Bill," *op. cit.*

expressed views. During the Wilson administration he had urged the entry of the federal government into ocean transportation. When the Senate in 1914 discussed governmental operation of Alaskan railroads, he offered an amendment calling for government operation and control of a shipping service which would be integrated with the government-owned Alaskan railroad. And after World War I he suggested that the merchant marine, constructed by the government during the war, be maintained and that the powers of the Panama Canal Company be enlarged to enable it to use these government-built and -owned ships rather than to sell them cheaply to private enterprise. Writing to a Nebraska voter, he stated his position: "I am very much in favor of the Government retaining its merchant marine. I would rather the Government would retain its ships and operate them, even though they do it at a loss, than to give them away to private persons and then pay a subsidy to those persons to operate them, and, in case of war, when we have to have the ships, buy them back again at a very much enhanced price." [38]

Norris believed that if the government operated these ships through the agency of the Panama Railway Company it would save many hundreds of millions of dollars that it would otherwise have to pay in exorbitant prices for freight. When the matter of subsidizing private shipping was under congressional consideration in the late 1920's, Norris reiterated his stand for government ownership. He declared in the Senate that "if we have to furnish the taxpayers' money to build the ships, then we ought to build them in the name of the taxpayers; and no private party can complain, because he admits that without getting a subsidy he would go out of business." [39]

The Norris transportation bill of 1924 was significant in a number of respects. Admittedly its methods for the financing of the corporation were sketchy and needed elaboration and refining, but that is a criticism of detail, not conception. The plan, intellectually congenial only to those who subscribed to the New Individualism espoused in Robert M. La Follette's 1924 Progressive party platform, was considered by the great majority to be the incarnation

[38] Norris to S. K. Warrick, February 26, 1923, Norris Papers.
[39] *Cong. Record*, 70th Cong., 1st sess. (May 16, 1928), Vol. 69, pt. 8, p. 8796. Norris, "If I Were President," *op. cit.*, p. 30.

of extreme radicalism. Even today such a bill, if proposed in the Senate, would raise cries of "regimentation," and "socialism." In the 1920's when the very concept of federal regulation was itself continually being challenged, the transportation bill was the quintescence of radicalism. Julius H. Barnes, president of the Chamber of Commerce of the United States, speaking for the business community, suggested, if not the complete abandonment of railroad regulation, then a regulatory policy of "utmost liberality." [40]

The Norris bill moved beyond regulation into public ownership and thus in pragmatic terms was completely beyond the pale of political acceptability. But although an ideological throwback to Populism, the bill was more advanced than Populist tenets and had much to commend it. (Norris always linked the transportation problem to the plight of the farmer; see below.) Most important, implicit in the bill was the recognition that transportation was a matter of public concern. Norris, unlike the Populists, thought beyond the mere correction or elimination of abuses, present or potential; he recognized the public character of transportation. The Nebraskan had moved from the belief that transportation was "quasi-public" in character to a realization of its full public import. Although nothing but defeat came of the bill, it was important to emphasize to the country the abstract right of the public. The bill also astutely recognized that land and water transportation were interconnected and interdependent, and that transportation was a national problem impinging directly on all facets of the economy. Furthermore, it extended the principle of the public or government corporation. Although government corporations had been used fairly extensively during World War I, Norris during the 1920's proposed to retain and utilize them for domestic peacetime needs. This extension of the function of the public corporation, in itself, is extremely important and the Senator deserves a great deal of credit for advocating it. And finally, the bill enunciated the yardstick principle subsequently carried over into the philosophy of the Tennessee Valley Authority. Norris believed that the establishment of a government corporation would provide both the public and the federal government with an adequate basis for determining whether or not the privately owned transportation

[40] James Warren Prothro, *The Dollar Decade: Business Ideas in the 1920's* (Baton Rouge: Louisiana State University Press, 1954), pp. 142–43.

companies were charging reasonable rates. The public transportation agency thus would compete with private rail and water lines, bringing about lower transportation prices, and if that failed, the government would then have adequate technical data for establishing a reasonable rate to be imposed on the private transportation companies.[41]

After the defeat of his 1924 transportation bill, Norris never engaged in any sustained battles for public ownership of transportation facilities. Another matter, however, was his belief, incorporated in the unsuccessful measure, that a government corporation should and could generate electrical power. The Nebraskan's monumental and ultimately successful struggle for the establishment of the TVA is chronicled below, but his rationale for this aspect of governmental ownership is related to the same premises which supported his arguments for public ownership of the transportation industry. Norris' concern with the development of water-power resources and the generation, transmission, and distribution of electrical energy, like his interest in public control of transportation, was based primarily on his belief that the public should be protected from the capricious whims of conscienceless gigantic corporations, dedicated only to the accumulation of enormous profits.

Electricity, he believed, occupied a special place in the pattern of modern life. America was entering the age of electricity, which was revolutionizing the social and economic conditions of all people. With its labor-saving qualities, electricity was a boon to all people, but it had special significance for the farmer in that it enabled him to combat nature on more nearly equal terms. All that was needed to give humanity the full enjoyment of this marvelous force was "to cheapen its production."

In a public address at Lincoln, Nebraska, the Senator outlined his view of the vital place which electricity occupied in American life and the role which the government should assume toward this essential utility.

[41] The First and Second Banks of the United States were the first notable early experiments with the public corporation. The public corporation, however, did not flourish until World War I when the Wilson administration established a number of public agencies to meet specific wartime needs. It was not until other crisis situations — the Great Depression and World War II — that the device of the public corporation again was utilized extensively.

Electricity is a necessity in every modern home. It is produced from our natural resources. Experience shows that its generation, transmission, and distribution can be brought about most economically and efficiently by monopoly. In fact, to get the best results, monopoly is essential. Assuming this to be true, I lay down the proposition that from its original generation to its final consumption by the consumer there should be no possibility of either private or corporation profit. It is similar to water in the modern home. It follows, therefore, there should be public generation, transmission, and distribution of electricity. No free people can permanently prosper or even endure, if a necessary element for human happiness or existence must be owned by private monopoly if that monopoly controls one of the natural resources God has given all his people. Electricity comes from our natural resources. Its economical development requires monopoly; it is a necessity of life, therefore, it should be supplied to our people without a profit to any person or private corporation from its generation, transmission, or distribution.[42]

However, the widest possible use of electricity was being denied to the people of the United States because of the evil activities of the "Power Trust." Throughout the 1920's Norris battled the Power Trust which he considered to be "one of the most corrupt monopolies which has ever existed." In his struggle against the power utilities he constantly emphasized the need for lower electric rates and more extensive service, particularly in rural areas. As a practical matter the Nebraskan advocated a government-operated superpower system which would get the maximum amount of electricity at a minimum cost. He envisioned such a system as capable of furnishing "heat and light and power to the people at cost." [43]

The Senator was not successful in his contest against the power monopoly, that "huge octopus on the road of human progress," but the passage of the Tennessee Valley Authority Act of 1933 inaugurated a new approach to the problem of federal regulation of electrical utilities. The TVA Act of 1933 authorized electrical service to farmer cooperatives, and two years later President Roosevelt created the Rural Electrification Administration by an

[42] George W. Norris, "Politics and Your Electricity Bills," reprinted from *Plain Talk* (July 1928), in *Cong. Record*, 71st Cong., 1st sess. (May 30, 1929), Vol. 71, pt. 2, p. 1521. George W. Norris, "A Finer Life on Nebraska Farms," Address at Lincoln, Nebraska, January 4, 1937, reprinted in *Cong. Record*, 75th Cong., 1st sess. (January 19, 1937), Vol. 81, pt. 9, p. 53.
[43] *Cong. Record*, 71st Cong., 1st sess. (May 30, 1929), Vol. 71, pt. 2, p. 1521. *Ibid.*, 75th Cong., 1st sess. (January 19, 1937), Vol. 81, pt. 9, p. 53.

executive order. Early in 1936, shortly after REA had gone into operation, Senator Norris introduced into the Senate a bill to make it permanent. A modified version of Norris' original measure passed the Senate that year and became known as the Norris-Rayburn Act.[44]

Although Nebraska is the nation's first and only all public power state and Norris has to his credit many national legislative achievements in his fight for cheap electricity, his major objective, a government-owned superpower system which would generate, transmit, and distribute electricity on a nonprofit basis to its users, is still as far from reality and public acceptance as was his ill-fated plan for government ownership of the means of transportation. In 1920 Senator Norris was fighting for the full resource development of the Potomac River. After repeated thwarting he cried out, "It is a moral sin that within the shadow of the dome of the Capitol one of the greatest waterpower possibilities is being wasted while we investigate and investigate." Today we are still investigating the possibilities of the Potomac, the Passamaquoddy, and others.[45]

Senator Norris wanted government operation of transportation and electric power because he could not "conceive of the monopoly of a necessary element of human existence being owned and controlled by private corporations for private gain." [46] If government would enter these two areas of natural monopoly and regulate other artificially created monopolies, free competition could then exist in the remainder of the economic sphere. This position, in which Norris attempted to protect the people and the interests of the state, was an advance over the unhampered free-competition doctrine of the laissez-faire school; but nonetheless, he held to an economic theory which to a large extent was a relic of the nine-

[44] Senator Norris' essential role in the creation of the Tennessee Valley Authority and his philosophy concerning its functions are discussed in Chapter Four. See also George W. Norris, *Fighting Liberal: The Autobiography of George W. Norris* (New York: The Macmillan Company, 1945). In a chapter entitled "Lighting the Farms," Norris discusses his role in the establishment of the Rural Electrification Administration.

[45] See Robert E. Firth, *Public Power in Nebraska: A Report on State Ownership* (Lincoln: University of Nebraska Press, 1962). Professor Firth details Norris' role in the establishment of public power in Nebraska. Clyde T. Ellis, "The Norris Mission: Key to the Western World," *Remarks Before the George W. Norris Centennial Conference* (Washington, D.C., May 16, 1961), p. 15.

[46] Norris to Paul S. Jacobsen, March 7, 1936, Norris Papers.

teenth century. His pathological fear of Big Business and the ogre of Wall Street arose because he accepted certain aspects of the doctrine of free competition. He believed in the basic necessity and virtue of the small entrepreneur and the small independent farmer. His advocacy of government regulation and government ownership and operation was his attempt to preserve the small atomistic unit in an economy which was moving in the direction of bigness and capital concentration. Government was to enter the economy to interdict the unbridled formation of trusts and monopolies with their tremendous capital concentration which upset the normal operations of a free-market economy. Thus, the Senator's support of both government ownership and his desire to perpetuate free competition, although seemingly an antimony, in actual fact was not a contradiction.

George W. Norris believed the role of the government was to promote the operation of a free economy and prevent the people from being economically oppressed. Thus, he recognized the need for governmental regulation or ownership in those areas of the economy which were affected with a high degree of public interest or were by their very nature natural monopolies. The function of government, in short, was to promote the general welfare through judicious interference in the economy. This conception of the welfare state was predicated on his inflexible belief that the fundamental purpose of government is to free the citizen from the haunting anxieties that destroy peace of mind and to bring to him the trinity of blessings proclaimed in the Declaration of Independence. The few should not have license to exploit the community in the name of liberty. Liberty and the democratic vision of the Good Life could only be achieved by positive government action.

☆　☆　☆　☆　☆　☆　☆　☆　☆

Democracy's Land and People

☆　☆　☆　☆　☆　☆　☆　☆　☆

AGRICULTURE

George William Norris, like so many other Americans since Thomas Jefferson, believed that the independent farmer epitomized the ethos of American democracy. As a child of the expanding frontier and later as a son of the Middle Border he was nurtured on an agrarian ideology which regarded agriculture as logically prior to all other economic activity. The permanent stability and security of agriculture were considerations of utmost concern to all citizens and to the government because the farmer "has made invaluable contributions to the design of American living, and of democratic government itself." [1] The Nebraskan cherished the ideal of a life lived close to the soil and nature, for in his opinion political democracy could not exist without an agrarian base. Agriculture possessed special virtues and was of national concern because it was the backbone of the American democratic faith and of all civilization.

Farming was indispensable to the material, psychological, and

[1] George W. Norris, *Fighting Liberal: The Autobiography of George W. Norris* (New York: The Macmillan Company, 1945), p. 372.

political welfare of all. If farming was not given its just share of the material rewards of American society, it was the obligation of the government to correct such an inequitable and harmful situation with positive action. Agriculture was entitled to government protection, not as charity, but as a matter of justice and right. The Senator always emphasized, and often rhapsodized, the central tenet of the agrarian myth that "it is at the rural fireside that virtue, morality, and patriotism have reached their highest state." [2] He accepted the fullest implications of the agrarian philosophy, "the foundation of all prosperity, and all security is land." [3]

Agriculture was the first industry; the farmer, the base of the economic pyramid, was first in importance because he fed and supported all other vocations and industries. One of the hardest working members of the population, denied the amenities of city living, the farmer was subject to the vicissitudes of both nature and the market. In a memorable address to the House of Representatives, the Nebraskan in florid phrases summarized his agrarian ideology:

We ought to legislate so that the tendency of going from the farm to the city will be reversed and make life in the country more enjoyable and more profitable, that the growing population of the cities may take advantage of this condition and move toward the farm. There is no doubt in the mind of any man but what it is desirable [sic] to have as large a rural population as possible. . . . Danger to our republican institutions will surely come if we legislate so as to decrease the rural population and drive the people into the already overcrowded cities. It is in the city, where the population is most dense, that there exists the most danger to the perpetuity of our institutions . . . it is also in the city that we have the slum and breeding places of anarchy, ignorance, and crime. It is there we have the mob. It is in the city that we have the machine politician and the political boss, where, by organization and machine control, the elective franchise is seriously interfered with. On the other hand, upon the farms are located the conservative, patriotic, and thinking voters of our country. Uninfluenced by the machine control or the political boss, they are the balance wheel of our form of government. In time of danger and in time of war we lean with

[2] U.S., *Congressional Record*, 58th Cong., 2d sess. (March 14, 1904), Vol. 38, pt. 4, p. 3257.
[3] *Ibid.*, 62d Cong., 2d sess. (July 5, 1912), Vol. 48, pt. 12, Appendix, p. 300. For an excellent description of the agrarian myth, see Richard Hofstadter, *The Age of Reform: From Bryan to F.D.R.* (New York: Alfred A. Knopf, 1956), pp. 23–46.

confidence and pride upon the strong arm and the willing and patriotic heart of the American farmer.[4]

The frontier was fading when Norris entered Nebraska local politics and by the time he came to Congress the promotion of agriculture was an accepted policy. For the better part of a century after the founding of the Republic, agriculture was the most important industry in the United States and absorbed the largest amount of capital and the largest working force. But by the beginning of the twentieth century the farm was forced to compete with the factory and government was compelled to recognize that the attenuation of an agricultural economy meant the adoption of new farm policies. (The Reclamation Act of 1902 signalized this significant change in American land policy.) As a freshman congressman, George W. Norris knew that the era of pioneer farming was nearing its close and that most of the nation's good farm land had come under private ownership, leaving only submarginal or exceedingly remote lands available for homesteading. The more fertile and productive valley lands had been settled and, in order to support a family, it had become necessary for the farmer to cultivate additional acres of the less productive remaining land. To make it easier for the family farmer, Congressman Norris outlined a plan to increase the homestead rights from the original 160 acres to 640 acres. This proposal ultimately was incorporated in the Kinkaid Act of 1904.[5]

When the 1910 census demonstrated that the population in the cities had been increasing and that the rural population, though still in the majority, was decreasing, the Nebraskan was exceedingly distressed. The cities were the cesspools of American society; it was of immediate concern to Congress to rectify this dangerous situation. The progressive perfection of American democracy could not continue unless the trend toward the cities was reversed. In order to perpetuate civic virtue and widen the agrarian base, Representative Norris, knowing that Wisconsin and Nebraska had just passed major legislation concerning cooperatives, introduced in the House a joint resolution to provide for the appointment of a

[4] *Cong. Record*, 61st Cong., 3d sess. (February 11, 1911), Vol. 46, pt. 5, Appendix, pp. 136–37.
[5] Murray R. Benedict, *Farm Policies of the United States, 1790–1950: A Study of Their Origins and Development* (New York: The Twentieth Century Fund, 1953), p. 126.

Farmers' National Cooperative Credit Commission which would investigate and report upon the plans and results of the German Raiffeisen system and all other European systems of rural coopera- tive credit associations. He hoped that some of these credit systems might be adaptable to conditions in the United States. Although well intentioned, the Norris Cooperative Credit Commission Reso- lution was not unique and it is exceedingly doubtful if it in any major way influenced the subsequent course of the American co- operative movement. Of considerably more significance were the earlier recommendations of President Theodore Roosevelt's Com- mission on Rural Life, which not only endorsed the cooperative principle but also specifically urged the states and the Congress to pass legislation promoting cooperatives.[6]

In 1916, after Congressional commissions had investigated Eu- ropean rural credit arrangements, the Federal Farm Loan Act was passed. Immediate plans for the rural cooperative movement, however, were never brought to fruition, primarily because shortly before and during World War I agriculture entered a period of inordinate prosperity. It was not until the farm depression of the 1920's that Norris' and other cooperative marketing plans were again given serious consideration.

The flush prosperity of the war years concealed the full dimen- sions of the agricultural problem which was to plague the nation during the lackluster Harding-Coolidge-Hoover era, when the farmers, suffering from a sharp inequality with other economic groups, sought in vain to improve their fundamental position. The agricultural depression which began in the summer and fall of 1920 and continued through the Great Depression — Nebraska farmers again burned corn for fuel as they had done in the bad days of Populism — was caused basically by a war-stimulated high production and a declining export market for basic crops. Specifi- cally, as John D. Hicks notes, "the removal of price guarantees as of May 31, 1920, the end of deficit financing, the unwillingness of the American government to continue foreign loans, the revival of European agriculture, and the increasing ability of other non-Eu- ropean nations to compete in the world's markets accounted prin- cipally for the ever lower prices at which American farmers were

[6] *Cong. Record*, 62d Cong., 2d sess. (July 5, 1912), Vol. 48, pt. 12, Appendix, p. 302.

obliged to sell." Furthermore, the nature of both consumption and farming was beginning to change. Millions of acres which formerly had been devoted to the growing of oats and other horse feed, now no longer needed for such crops because of increasing mechanization, were freed for commercial crop production.[7] When President Harding failed to offer a satisfactory agricultural program to meet the growing challenge of the agricultural depression, Senator Norris, in May 1921, joined with senators of both parties from the dominantly agricultural states to help create a loose congressional organization which rapidly became known as the farm bloc.[8] To many, at the time, the formation of the farm bloc was thought to be a dangerous departure and a threat to the traditional two-party system. Events, however, soon proved otherwise. Despite the outward manifestation of solidarity, attachment to the farm bloc fluctuated from issue to issue, for among its members there were wide divergencies in ideology. Thus, for example, Senators Norris of Nebraska, La Follette of Wisconsin, and Ladd of North Dakota had little more in common with Senators Kellogg of Minnesota, Swanson of Virginia, and Capper of Kansas than sympathy for agriculture.[9]

The other members of the farm bloc, along with Norris, shared

[7] John D. Hicks, *Rehearsal for Disaster: The Boom and Collapse of 1919–1920* (Gainesville: University of Florida Press, 1961), p. 77.
[8] See Benedict, *op. cit.*, p. 181. Those in attendance at the initial meeting of the farm bloc, in addition to Norris, were: Kenyon of Iowa, Kendrick of Wyoming, Gooding of Idaho, Capper of Kansas, Smith of South Carolina, Fletcher of Florida, La Follette of Wisconsin, Sheppard of Texas, Ladd of North Dakota, Ransdell of Louisiana, and Heflin of Alabama. The number of members belonging to the bloc varied. The effective number in the Senate at any one time probably was not more than twenty-six or twenty-seven. In the House there were ninety-five or ninety-six strong supporters plus a score more who were sympathetic. Tactics varied; the Senate bloc usually held regular meetings at which cabinet members and experts spoke. The House group utilized key men on committees and in state delegations. Theodore Saloutos and John D. Hicks, *Agricultural Discontent in the Middle West, 1900–1939* (Madison: University of Wisconsin Press, 1951), p. 324. Writing two decades after its creation Wesley McCune has commented, "The notion that the farm bloc is a group of willful Western and Southern Congressmen is a fallacy. When a legislative crisis impends it is the votes of congressmen from Eastern and Northern states, who also have rural constituents, that put the farm bloc over to its accustomed victory." Wesley McCune, *The Farm Bloc* (Garden City, New York: Doubleday, Doran and Company, Inc., 1943), p. 1.
[9] James H. Shideler, *Farm Crisis: 1919–1923* (Berkeley and Los Angeles: University of California Press, 1957), p. 156.

the basic assumption that the prosperity of agriculture was fundamental to the prosperity of the nation and that it was imperative to raise agriculture to a status of equality with industry and other groups in the population. The Nebraskan scoffed at charges that the formation of the farm bloc created an unholy alliance which sought to extort special privileges from the government. The farm bloc, he claimed, was a necessary protective measure because the railroads, the trusts, and all other forms of big business were in "dirty politics . . . spreading propaganda from one end of the country to another." The ills of the farmer were, to a large extent, "caused by legislation or unequal application of laws." [10] The inescapable alternative was to seek relief through legislative action.

Throughout the twelve Republican years of Harding, Coolidge, and Hoover, the Senator constantly dunned the Administration to take corrective action to aid the farmer. He correctly believed that the serious farm situation was not of the farmers' creation; it had not arisen because of the farmers' neglect or inability. The ultimate solution to the problem resided in the larger economic sphere. "Politics and economics," Norris knowledgeably affirmed, "meet more often and more closely than is usually conceded, and political action can help to solve" the agricultural distresses.[11]

Senator Norris' rationale for government aid to the depressed farmers and his proposed plans for amelioration were predicated on his understanding of the causes of the agricultural depression. Essentially he believed that the trouble with agriculture could be reduced to three elements: first, the tariff — the farmer did not get the benefit of the protective tariff; second, the farm surplus — the farmer, unlike the manufacturer, could not limit his production and consequently cultivated more edibles than could be consumed in the United States; and third, the cost of distribution —"between the producer and the consumer there is a multitude of middlemen, who neither toil nor spin and yet make enormous profits upon the food products of the country as such products travel from the producer to the consumer." [12]

[10] George W. Norris, "Why the Farm Bloc," *The World Tomorrow*, II (June 1928), 257–58.
[11] *Ibid.*, p. 256.
[12] George W. Norris, "The Farmers' Situation, a National Danger," *Current History*, XXIV (April 1926), 10.

Norris was concerned about the problem of giving the farmer the benefit of the tariff enjoyed by the manufacturer and the laborer. Acknowledging that tariff protection was a nationalistic device based on the theory that the American standard of living was higher than that of other nations, he boldly assumed that the United States "must maintain that difference in the standard of living by a protective tariff." [13] If it was just, he reasoned, to levy a tariff on manufactured goods in order to enable factory owners to pay higher wages to their workers, then the farmer ought not to be compelled to buy what he consumes in a protected market, yet sell what he produces in a free-trade market. The farmer buys inside the tariff wall and is forced to sell outside it; the prices of his purchases are fixed, but the prices of his agricultural sales are subject to dictation by the markets of the world. It is unjust for the farmer to have to sell his surplus in a world market which can depress the price of his products.[14]

The farmer is a consumer, like other elements of the population, and is subject to the same increase in the cost of things he purchases. The manufacturer, the Senator contended, can increase his selling price until it is raised to the level of the tariff barrier, which means that the industrialist meets no competition from the foreign manufacturer unless he raises his price above the tariff. This added cost is passed to the retailer, who in turn passes it to the consumer. "If the consumer be a laboring man," Norris wrote in *The Nation*, "the additional price that he pays is to some extent reflected in a higher wage, but when it reaches the farmer it stops. He cannot pass the additional burden to someone else." [15] If the tariff enabled the farmer to add the duty to the selling price of his produce he would then be able, in part, to meet his additional cost. The agricultural surplus, however, must find a market in the trade centers of the world in competition with produce grown at a lower cost.

But basically, the Senator felt that industry was overprotected. He was willing to grant the benefits of protection only on the condition "that every rank in the social strata of America may get

[13] George W. Norris, "The Tariff and the Farmer," *The Nation*, CXXIII (September 1, 1926), 192.
[14] Norris, "The Farmers' Situation," *op. cit.*, p. 11.
[15] Norris, "The Tariff and the Farmer," *op. cit.*, p. 192.

the benefit of it equally." [16] He feared the consequences of over-protection, not only for the farmer, but also for the consumer. "One of the dangers," he maintained "that follows the levying of a high-protective tariff is that it enables the producers and the manufac-turers of the article upon which the tariff is levied, this side of the tariff wall, to form combinations and monopolies, and thus exact unfair and unjust prices from the consumer." [17]

The difficulties of arriving at an equitable tariff were com-pounded by the existence of the second interrelated element of the farm problem — the agricultural surplus. Prior to the New Deal agricultural legislation the Senator firmly believed that "the farmer can not limit his production like the manufacturer." [18] It was neces-sary for the farmer to cultivate to the limit of his energy, for he could not know in advance whether nature would enable him to reap a large or a small crop. He did not know if there would be a surplus or a shortage, and it often occurred that the farmer was financially better off when there was a shortage. Furthermore, the farmer was, in general, in the untenable situation in which "his business is so unprofitable that he is nearly aways compelled to borrow money to produce a crop, and to a great extent he is then subject to the control of the man or the institution that holds the mortgage." [19]

The third problem facing agriculture, Norris believed, was the high cost of distribution paid by the farmer. "As the product

[16] *Cong. Record*, 71st Cong., 1st sess. (October 18, 1929), Vol. 71, pt. 4, p. 4671.

[17] *Ibid.*, 71st Cong., 2d sess. (March 20, 1930), Vol. 72, pt. 6, p. 5689. Norris' concern for the welfare of the public ultimately crystallized itself into an amendment to the 1930 tariff act. The amendment attempted to protect the consumer by establishing an Office of People's Counsel and also by per-mitting any citizen to file a complaint in the Customs Court. Should the Court after taking evidence on the complaint find the charge substantiated, then "it shall be the duty of the President within one month to issue a procla-mation suspending the imposition and collection of the duty or duties levied . . . upon such article." In arguing for his amendment the Senator expressed his rationale quite succinctly: "No manufacturer, no producer, is entitled to a protective tariff as a matter of right. It is a legislative favor; and when the object of levying a protective tariff is circumvented by the beneficiaries of the protective tariff and monopolies are formed and unjust prices demanded it is not only the right but the duty of the Government that gives those favors under such circumstances to take them away." *Ibid.*

[18] Norris, "The Farmers' Situation," *op. cit.*, p. 11.

[19] *Ibid.*, p. 12.

travels from the producer to the consumer it goes through the hands of too many middlemen, each one of whom exacts his profit, sometimes an exorbitant and unreasonable one." [20] A key factor in the excessive cost of marketing was the railroad trust which operated a freight rate system which charged as much as the traffic would bear. The excessive freight rates, the Nebraskan charged in arguments reminiscent of earlier agrarian dissent movements, is in itself sufficient to wreck any industry; and when the industry is operating in depressed circumstances, or on a marginal basis, the freight rate assumes critical proportions. The farmer is harassed by dual freight charges; "the freight is added to everything which he buys," Norris asserted, "and it is deducted from everything which he sells." [21] In an article for *The Nation* the Senator pointed out that

the railroad is perhaps the greatest of all middlemen. . . . Its freight revenue is acquired by a levy upon the products of human consumption as they travel from the producer to the consumer . . . the farmer has a greater interest in the freight question than any other class. All dealers, from the manufacturer down to the consumer, add the price of freight to the commodity they handle. When it reaches the farmer he has no opportunity to pass the increase on. He is at the end of the equation and therefore must absorb it. On the other hand, when he has anything to sell the freight charge is immediately deducted from his return. The price of his wheat at the farm is the Chicago or Minneapolis price, less the freight. The cost of his plow or his harrow or his clothes or anything else he has to buy is the manufacturer's price plus the middleman's profit, and always plus the freight. Thus he pays the freight twice, and he is the only class of our citizens who does this.[22]

Norris was concerned not only because others prospered, but also because the masters of finance and industry were indifferent to the farmers' plight. "When the great leaders of banking and industry can see no further than the artificial prosperity that comes to Big Business while those who toil on farms are getting no return for their labor, then indeed we have a right to question the wisdom of our financial leaders." [23]

Beginning in the early 1920's and continuing to the New Deal,

[20] George W. Norris, "If I Were President" (unpublished MS, n.d.), p. 27, Norris Papers.
[21] Norris, "The Farmers' Situation," *op. cit.*, p. 10.
[22] Norris, "The Tariff and the Farmer," *op. cit.*, p. 193.
[23] Norris, "The Farmers' Situation," *op. cit.*, p. 10.

Norris began introducing legislation designed to aid agriculture. In the late spring of 1921 he urged the passage of a bill creating an Agricultural Foreign Trade Financing Corporation. This corporation, with a capital stock of $50 million, would be established to finance the sale of surplus crops abroad. The capital would be advanced by the government from the profits of the United States Grain Corporation and there would be an authorization under the bill to issue and sell debentures up to $500 million. Loans would be granted to farmers on long-term credits so that their crops could be shipped to foreign markets. The farmers in turn would be required to purchase from the corporation capital stock in the amount of 10 per cent of the value of their exports. Hopefully the Senator believed that, through this scheme, the farmers in a year or two would own the business and the government would have received the money lent from the Grain Corporation funds to start the agricultural financing corporation.[24]

In June 1921, Norris' proposals were embodied in a bill for the creation of the Federal Farmers' Export Financing Corporation which would buy farm products in the United States and sell them abroad. The Norris bill initially received the farm bloc support, but Secretary of Commerce Herbert Hoover and Secretary of Agriculture Henry C. Wallace refused to support the measure. While hearings on the bill were in progress, President Harding sent a message to Congress suggesting that the War Finance Corporation be authorized to take care of agricultural needs through enlarged capital for financing exports. Administration pressures resulted in the substitution of this proposal, the Kellogg Amendment, for the Norris bill, and the farm bloc reluctantly went along with it.[25]

Senator Norris, exceedingly unhappy about the substitution, grudgingly supported it because it was better "than no bill at all." However, there was a fundamental difference between the Kellogg measure and the Norris measure in that the corporation provided for by the Nebraskan would have been a link between the producer and the consumer while the new bill failed to provide such a link. Norris acidly observed that the Kellogg bill was sharp prac-

---

[24] *New York Times*, May 16, 1921, 26:4. *Ibid.*, June 1, 1921, 16:8. See also George W. Norris, "Farmers' Export Finance Corporation Act," *Senate Report No. 192*, 67th Cong., 1st sess. (Washington, D.C.: Government Printing Office, June 30, 1921).
[25] Benedict, *op. cit.*, p. 183.

tice, since it dealt with "bankers, with middlemen, with trust companies, and confers all favors upon them." [26] The Nebraskan was forever skeptical about "farmers who have viewed the crops from the twentieth story of a building on Wall Street." [27] The wisdom of hindsight shows that the Norris measure had little prospect of being passed by Congress or accepted by the Administration; in addition to being exceedingly crude and general, it committed the government to direct participation in agricultural production and marketing.

Now aware that the Republican administration would emasculate any suggestions for positive subsidization of agriculture, Norris again turned his attention to agricultural remedies based on the principle of cooperative marketing. In December 1922, he introduced a bill ambitiously designed to "provide a market for the sale of agricultural products, and to eliminate as far as possible the commissions and charges that are exacted upon agricultural products from the time such products leave the producer until same reaches the consumer, and to thereby increase the price which the producer receives and decrease the price which the consumer pays." These objectives, the Senator believed, could be achieved by establishing a government corporation with a capital stock of $100 million to be contributed entirely by the government. The corporation, controlled by a board of three directors appointed by the President by and with the advice and consent of the Senate, would have had the following powers: (1) to build, buy, lease, and operate elevators and storage warehouses; (2) to buy agricultural products from any firm or corporation, or cooperative organization in financing the sale, or exportation and sale of such agricultural products.[28] However, the Norris bill was speedily rejected.

In the winter of 1923–24 there was a revival of interest in the export corporation idea previously embodied in the Norris bill of 1921. For the special session of the Sixty-seventh Congress, Norris, with the assistance of Louis Crossette, confidential adviser to Herbert Hoover, and Carl Vrooman, Assistant Secretary of Agriculture under President Wilson, prepared new legislation. The new

[26] *Cong. Record*, 67th Cong., 1st sess. (July 28, 1921), Vol. 61, pt. 5, p. 4379.
[27] *Ibid.*, 67th Cong., 1st sess. (July 28, 1921), Vol. 61, pt. 5, p. 4381.
[28] *Ibid.*, 67th Cong., 4th sess. (December 19, 1922), Vol. 64, pt. 1, p. 666.

bill, now called the Norris-Sinclair bill, received a favorable report from the powerful Senate Committee on Agriculture and Forestry, of which Norris was chairman, but never secured passage in the Senate. The Norris-Sinclair bill utilized the device of a government corporation to be financed through government funds. The corporation would have power to purchase agricultural and manufactured products in this country and sell them under generous terms of credit abroad. A board was to be created to administer the affairs of the corporation with the Secretary of Commerce to be the *ex officio* chairman of the board and have general charge of the business of the corporation. Herbert Hoover, then Secretary of Commerce, would automatically have been in charge. The bill also provided that the merchant marine built during World War I by the U.S. Shipping Board (and now rotting in idleness along the eastern seaboard) should be turned over to the corporation free of cost. The only conditions attached to the transfer of ships were that the corporation keep them in reasonable repair and surrender them to the government on demand. The Interstate Commerce Commission was to have authority to reduce rates upon all products dealt in by this corporation from the place of purchase to the point of exportation. Norris also included in the bill a provision that products sold on time should be paid for by debentures issued by the purchaser. These debentures were to be sold for cash and the cash in turn used to purchase more goods, thus enabling a stable practical period of operation.[29]

By using Herbert Hoover as a symbol of respectability and conservatism, Norris attempted to stifle the charge that such a corporation would be an excessive governmental interference in the economy, but he was unsuccessful. James H. Shideler has noted that "it was not necessary for the Republican Party leadership to use its influence against the bill so long as southern Democrats were repelled by Norris' 'socialism'."[30] The Republican slogan "Less government in business" carried the day.

The Norris-Sinclair bill was countered by the McNary-Haugen movement which was the central farm legislation issue from 1924 to 1928. Norris always felt that the McNary-Haugen plan did not

---

[29] George W. Norris, "Agricultural Export Bill," *Senate Report No. 193*, 68th Cong., 1st sess. (Washington D.C.: Government Printing Office, March 5, 1924).
[30] Shideler, *op. cit.*, p. 241.

get to the heart of the farm problem and would "not furnish a real remedy for the situation." Yet he supported it rather than have no remedial farm legislation pass.[31] The basic principle of all five McNary-Haugen bills that came under congressional considera-tion involved the concept of a government export corporation which would purchase agricultural commodities on a scale suffi-cient to raise the domestic price to a defined "ratio-price" which would then create a situation of "equality for agriculture." [32] The corporation, in short, was to subsidize the export of basic commodi-ties so as to raise prices to a parity level. The costs of subsidized export were to be charged to producers through the equalization fee, and the parity-price goal was defined as a system of prices that would bear substantially the same relationship to the all-com-modities index as prices of those commodities bore to that index during the prewar period 1905–14.[33]

In 1927 and 1928 the McNary-Haugen bills passed Congress, but were vetoed by President Coolidge on both occasions. In opposing the McNary-Haugen bills Coolidge maintained that the government should not engage in buying and selling farm com-modities; such action, he philosophized, was repugnant to Ameri-ca's commercial and political institutions. Coolidge's strong vetoes tossed the farm problem into the 1928 presidential campaign.

Like Coolidge, Hoover too denounced the McNary-Haugen equalization-fee principle, but he promised to aid agriculture through cooperative marketing. Hoover and other Republicans had committed themselves to cooperative marketing, not because they were dedicated to it, but because, of all the numerous reme-dies advanced to help agriculture, cooperative marketing was the least offensive to the large industrial interests. Despite the motiva-tion, or lack of it, "the aid given the cooperatives by the Republi-cans," Saloutos and Hicks report, "was one of the few achievements of the otherwise lethargic administrations of Harding, Coolidge, and Hoover." [34]

After the election, Herbert Hoover called a special session of

[31] *Cong. Record*, 67th Cong., 4th sess. (February 2, 1923), Vol. 64, pt. 3, p. 2895. Norris, "Why the Farm Bloc," *op. cit.*, p. 257.
[32] Benedict, *op. cit.*, p. 212. The phrase "equality for agriculture" was orig-inally developed and publicized by George N. Peek and Hugh S. Johnson of the Moline Plow Company.
[33] Shideler, *op. cit.*, p. 275.
[34] Saloutos and Hicks, *op. cit.*, p. 290.

Congress in the spring of 1929 in order to remedy agrarian distress with the tariff structure. When the Agricultural Marketing Act of 1929 was before the Senate, Norris vainly struggled to include in it an export-debenture amendment which essentially was a modified version of the equalization fee of the McNary-Haugen plan. Although the Administration was against it, the Senate accepted the export-debenture feature, but it was lost at the insistence of the House in the conference committee. The Nebraskan criticized the Farm Board because "it failed disastrously in its attempt to sell the surplus which it had purchased." [35] However, Norris failed to realize that the Farm Board experiment had been initiated during a time of deteriorating agricultural economic conditions and of growing world surpluses or that the Agricultural Marketing Act of 1929 was, in the words of Saloutos and Hicks, "the most important single piece of legislation ever enacted in behalf of cooperative marketing." [36]

In 1932 Norris again proposed a debenture program similar to the one he had introduced in the Agricultural Marketing Act of 1929. This suggestion, embodied as an amendment to the tariff legislation, was defeated.[37] This defeat marked the end of Norris' struggles with the Republican administrations over the farm problem.

With the coming of the Roosevelt administration, the Nebraskan's direct sponsorship of agricultural legislation ceased. This may be because he felt that the farmers would henceforth receive an equitable hearing by the Administration and because he began concentrating most of his energies on the TVA and problems related to its extension. Although not in complete accord with FDR's agricultural policy (particularly when it attempted to reduce surpluses by destroying them), he developed a permissive attitude toward it. He realized that the extent of the general Depression was so overwhelming that it was necessary for him to support whatever action programs the New Deal devised.

Norris unblushingly subscribed to an agrarian ideal and its values, when both the ideal and the values were being subjected

[35] George W. Norris, "The Eagle or the Parrot" (unpublished MS, n.d.), p. 8, Norris Papers.
[36] Saloutos and Hicks, *op. cit.*, p. 290.
[37] *Cong. Record*, 72d Cong., 1st sess. (May 24, 1932), Vol. 75, pt. 10, p. 10982.

to the heavy critical pressures of a society which was rapidly becoming industrialized and urbanized. He appreciated and understood the needs and desires of the dirt farmer. But his affection and nostalgia for the family farmer blinded him to the realization that the advance of a new technology was rapidly making obsolete the family farm while giving rise to the factory farm. Norris, like most farm spokesmen of the twenties, refused to come to grips with the ever more apparent fact that agriculture was steadily diminishing in importance in the social and political scene. Norris could not conceive, and would not have wanted to, of huge impersonal factories in the fields. To him they would be the antithesis of the yeoman farmer; they connoted not honest industry, hard work, economic independence, and equality built on close contact with the soil, but rather, impersonal exploitation by a heartless corporation which had no reverence for nature and was only concerned with growing crops of profits to be eaten by the already overfat absentee stockholder. Though Norris' enthusiasm for the yeoman farmer was genuine, it was based upon emotion rather than logic. He mistakenly believed that the values of the agrarian society could best be achieved by fostering an agricultural economy which was steadily losing its viability.

Senator Norris' understanding of the causes of the agricultural depression were hardly sophisticated and were markedly populistic in that he laid much of the blame on the railroads and other middlemen. Furthermore, his comprehension of the scope of foreign forces on the domestic agricultural market was limited. But Norris' fundamental error was his failure to see that agriculture is not a simple homogeneous unit of the economy and society. He failed to recognize that agriculture encompasses many different groups with many different problems. His solutions to the farm problem, although honestly motivated, could not have slackened the inexorable exodus from the farm. Both the defects and the virtues of his farm philosophy stem from his uncritical acceptance of the agrarian myth. While his advocacy of governmental support for farmers because of their fundamental economic position is logic subject to question, his support for farmers as people — as hungry, tired people with many problems and needs — is to his enduring credit.

Other important things also innure to his credit. Norris never was pro-farmer at the expense of the laborer and the other consumers. He advocated agricultural aid, not as a venal lobbyist, or as one thinking solely of his constituency interests, but because he sincerely believed that by helping the farmer the nation would be helped. He realistically acknowledged that his farm programs were "subject to the criticism that to some extent it puts the Government in business." [38] He recognized that, even with farm bloc support, his programs were never politically palatable for the business-oriented administrations of the 1920's. The Senator advocated a marketing corporation, which would serve as a huge middleman, for the high purpose of performing economical marketing services and not for making profits. It was a well-formed plan to enlist urban support for farm relief and was in tune with his vision of progressive economic reform. His other programs, recognizing the depth of the problem, required government intervention and help. However, the large-scale positive action to aid agriculture which Norris recommended did not take place until the New Deal. But Norris' continued efforts on behalf of agriculture during the 1920's conditioned the country to the fact that effective aid to agriculture required some form of governmental intervention in the free market. These efforts ultimately bore fruit beginning with the New Deal. Norris' efforts and his failures are more important for United States market agricultural policy than is his direct legislative accomplishment of altering the marketing structure in behalf of agriculture.

LABOR

George William Norris was interested in labor as well as agriculture and recognized the interdependence of farm and factory. Although a prosperous agriculture was a requisite for a flourishing democracy, that in itself was insufficient; it was also axiomatic that democracy could not long exist if the great mass of the labor force were oppressed and discontented. Norris extended to labor as well as to agriculture the ethical imperative that it was entitled to a fair return for its toil. He fervently believed that "the farmers and the laborers ought to be together . . . they are fighting the same battle" to achieve the American democratic vision.[39] It was

[38] Norris, "The Farmers' Situation," *op. cit.*, p. 12.
[39] Norris to Edward Keating, August 5, 1929, Norris Papers.

essential that the laborer have an opportunity to work in an atmosphere that reflected the dignity of his toil. Like the farmer, the laborer was subject to the conditions which he as an atomistic unit in an unbalanced market society could not control, and was, therefore, entitled to the protection of positive government.

It was during the twenties that Norris first became aware of the needs of labor. Along with the farmers the workers failed to share equitably in the material advantages of this period. Both the farmer and the laborer felt adversely, and disproportionately, the serious maladjustments within the economy. There was, furthermore, a reciprocal relationship within this imbalance. The economic paradox of the new economic era, rural depression amid relative urban prosperity, contributed to a population shift which greatly affected labor. The trend from rural to urban existence — the lure of the city — which Norris and others had so ominously noted a decade before, accelerated sharply. Between 1920 and 1930 the farm population declined by 3.7 per cent (31.6 to 30.4 million) while the non-farm population increased by 24.6 per cent (74.1 million to 92.3 million). "Never before," writes labor historian Irving Bernstein, "had the United States experienced such an immense flow from farm to city." [40]

Correlated to the farm increase in the work force was the curtailment of the supply of immigrant labor. In 1917, despite President Wilson's logical and articulate veto, Congress fundamentally reversed America's traditional policy of almost unrestricted immigration by enacting a literacy requirement for aliens seeking admission to the United States. The literacy test, designed to discriminate against southern and eastern Europeans, was buttressed by the national origins quota principle first enacted in 1921 and made permanent in 1924. These restrictions markedly reduced the total number of immigrants and established (on the basis of the national origins quota) a distribution favorable to the British Isles, Germany, and Scandinavia.

These changes within the pattern of the labor force were occurring simultaneously with rapid technological advances and increasing mechanization. Productivity increased but the number of man-hours required per unit of output decreased. For the

[40] Irving Bernstein, *The Lean Years: A History of the American Worker 1920–1933* (Boston: Houghton Mifflin Company, 1960), p. 48.

worker, technological change bred income inequality, a relatively low standard of living, and often tragic unemployment. Norris recognized this and also that temporary technological unemployment presented a serious problem to some industries. Nevertheless, the Senator urged labor to accept the introduction of technology and use it to the benefit of labor. In the long run, he reasoned, the worker would gain by the introduction of mechanization and automation. "Any man who stands in the way of human progress and seeks to prevent the use of technological improvements," he reflected in his Autobiography, "is standing in his own way and blocking his own progress." [41] The Nebraskan recognized that "labor cannot afford to place itself in an attitude of opposition to invention, to human progress, and to improvement." [42]

Despite the "golden glow" of the 1920's there was serious and persistent unemployment, ranging, Foster Rhea Dulles reports, "in terms of man-years from ten to thirteen per cent of the total labor supply." Even in the good year of 1928 some two million persons were probably without jobs. The Lynds, in their brilliant study of Middletown, discovered that, despite the prosperity of the community, the fear of being laid off was constant among the working-class families.[43]

Immediately after the brief economic collapse of 1921, Norris, recognizing the unevenness in the economy, had proposed in the Senate that the government "take steps to relieve unemployment in times of depression by constructing public works." [44] He even suggested that it would be advisable to prepare for the possibility of a depression by enacting a law enabling the President to initiate public projects in order to maintain a fully employed labor force. The use of federal funds, the Senator believed, should be expended for the improvement of rivers and harbors, the erection of public buildings, the development of water power projects, and "even the building of homes for laborers and disposing of them on time, almost anything that would bring employment." [45]

[41] Norris, *Fighting Liberal, op. cit.*, p. 266.
[42] Norris to Edward Keating, July 24, 1929, Norris Papers.
[43] Foster Rhea Dulles, *Labor in America* (New York: Thomas Y. Crowell Company, 1949), p. 244.
[44] *Cong. Record*, 67th Cong., 2d sess. (February 16, 1922), Vol. 62, pt. 3, p. 2651.
[45] *Ibid.*

This urging of the national government to intervene in the economic order in order to promote full employment, long before the Great Depression scarred the economy and society and before the New Deal popularized the Keynesian concepts of pump-priming, represented a truly advanced attitude. The inexorable logic of Norris' position, starkly emphasized by the corrosive tragedy of the Depression, was vindicated and ultimately received a modest fruition twenty-five years later with the passage of the Employment Act of 1946. Now it is not only a legal duty, but also part of the conventional expectations of the public that the President will attempt to maintain a healthy economy, avoid economic fluctuations, maintain employment, production, and purchasing power.

Although Norris never lived to see his anti-depression formulae become legislation, he, nonetheless, had the satisfaction of knowing that he had contributed major legislation to the healthy, orderly development of unionism in the United States. The Norris-LaGuardia Act of 1932, called by Archibald Cox "the first of the four statutory cornerstones of the current national labor policy," [46] remains as a monument to the Nebraskan's recognition of the significance of the labor movement's participation in achieving a more democratic America. The Federal Anti-Injunction Act, finally enacted at the nadir of the Great Depression after a roiled legislative history, had practical social, economic, and political origins.

The contemporary forces conditioning the Norris-LaGuardia Act and the subsequent evolution of federal interest in labor-management relations began a full decade before the twentieth century with the passage of the eventful Sherman Antitrust Act. The Sherman Act of 1890, a law whose intentions as applied to labor were ambiguous and controversial, had a genesis in congressional desire to restrict trusts and the monopoly of capital which characterized the American post–Civil War era of rapid industrial expansion. The Sherman Act, as simple in statement as it was complex in interpretation and application, elevated to legislative importance the venerable common-law doctrine of conspiracy. The Act ambitiously proclaimed that "every contract, combination in the form of trust or otherwise, or conspiracy, in restraint of trade or commerce among the several states, or with foreign nations, is

[46] Archibald Cox, *Law and the National Labor Policy* (Los Angeles: Institute of Industrial Relations, University of California, 1960), p. 4.

hereby declared to be illegal." Federal courts received jurisdiction to enforce it, the Attorney General was empowered to secure injunctive relief and initiate criminal prosecutions against violators, and injured persons were permitted to sue the lawbreakers for triple damages.[47]

Despite its overwhelming passage (the vote was 52 to 1 in the Senate and 242 to 0 in the House), little enthusiasm was evinced for it during the Harrison, Cleveland, and McKinley administrations. "From 1898 to 1901, when new combinations were being formed at a rate never equalled before or since, the sole suit instituted by the government concerned a relatively minor coal-and-coke pool." [48] Initial efforts to dissolve the monolithic trusts were lackadaisical and, not too surprisingly, dismally unsuccessful. Successful application of the Sherman Act, however, ironically occurred when applied to labor. In 1893 and 1894, lower courts in minor cases interpreted the Antitrust Act as applying to unions and granted injunctions against strikes. This again occurred during the Pullman Strike of 1894, when Boston corporation lawyer Richard Olney, then U.S. Attorney General, obtained a sweeping injunction against militant Eugene V. Debs and other determined leaders of the American Railway Union for conspiring to restrain trade and interfere with the mails. The lower courts upheld the injunction squarely on the Sherman Act, but the Supreme Court, choosing to be more equivocal, based its affirmance on broader grounds.

In 1895, the same year that the Supreme Court decided *In re Debs*, it temporarily emasculated the Sherman Act's application to industrial combinations when it held that the sugar trust, then controlling 98 per cent of the domestic refining industry, did not constitute a monopoly in violation of the commerce clause because the manufacture of sugar was not in interstate commerce! During the same term the Court held that taxes derived from land or personal property were direct and thus, since they were not apportioned among the states according to population, were unconstitutional.

[47] Charles O. Gregory, *Labor and the Law* (New York: W. W. Norton and Company, Inc., 1946), p. 201.
[48] Merle Fainsod, Lincoln Gordon, and Joseph C. Palamountain, Jr., *Government and the American Economy* (New York: W. W. Norton and Company, Inc., 1959), p. 450.

It was not until the ratification of the Sixteenth Amendment in 1913 that this decision was overruled.

These adamant laissez-faire pronouncements by the courts were but harbingers of future union repression. In 1908 the Supreme Court handed down the Danbury Hatters' decision which provoked consternation in labor's ranks. Some six years before, in a campaign for the closed shop, the United Hatters of North America struck and declared a nationwide boycott against the products of Danbury, Connecticut, hat manufacturer D. E. Loewe and Company. In retaliation, the manufacturer helped organize the American Anti-Boycott Association and sued the union for triple damages under the Sherman Act. Upholding the lower courts, the Supreme Court unequivocally held that the Act made "no distinction between classes." The boycott, thus, was a conspiracy in restraint of trade and the union was liable. Labor officials realized that the effect of this ruling was to establish the doctrine that all strike activities were within the purview of federal courts and that defiance of injunctions would result in fines, loss of property, and even imprisonment. The specter now rose that unions might be harassed into dissolution. The excessive fear of labor proved unfounded, although between 1908 and 1914 the Sherman Act was invoked against unions in more than fifteen cases in inferior federal courts.[49]

During the time when judicial interference and interdiction of union activity was being crystallized, labor was engaged in a campaign to secure relief from injunctions and the application of the Sherman Act. Beginning in 1906 organized labor embarked on political activity. They presented to President Theodore Roosevelt and Congress a Bill of Grievances which specifically demanded relief from judicial interference and the revision of the Sherman Act. These demands were emphasized when labor entered the 1906 congressional campaign and helped elect six union members to the House of Representatives. Two years later, Samuel Gompers presented the American Federation of Labor's demands to the platform committees of the Republican and Democratic national conventions. The Republicans refused to acknowledge labor's claims, but the Democrats adopted a plank which, in typical platform verbiage, paid lip service to the courts as the "bulwark of

[49] Bernstein, *op. cit.*, p. 207.

our liberties" and then went on to affirm that "labor organizations and their members should not be regarded as illegal combinations in restraint of trade."[50] Gompers and his colleagues acknowledged the positions of the parties and actively supported the ill-fated candidacy of twice-defeated William Jennings Bryan. The 1908 Democratic defeat, however, was but a temporary setback for labor. Four years later, the Democrats reaffirmed their pledge to labor, and labor again campaigned for the Democrats. With the Republican vote badly split, Woodrow Wilson captured the presidency and the Democrats won control of Congress.

The political climate now favored labor. The new Secretary of Labor, William B. Wilson, was a former high official of the United Mine Workers; union members now in the House of Representatives had increased to fifteen.[51] In 1914, after a tortured legislative session, labor organizations finally prevailed upon Congress to include in the Clayton Antitrust Act an amendment to the Sherman Act interdicting certain corporate practices, and a number of provisions which the unions believed would remove labor activities from the purview of the hated antitrust legislation. Accordingly, the famous section 6 of the Clayton Act declared

> that the labor of a human being is not a commodity or an article of commerce. Nothing contained in the antitrust laws shall be construed to forbid the existence and operation of labor, agricultural, or horticultural organizations, instituted for the purposes of mutual help, and not having capital stock or conducted for profit, or to forbid or restrain individual members of such organizations from lawfully carrying out the legitimate objects thereof; nor shall such organizations, or the members thereof, be held or construed to be illegal combinations or conspiracies in restraint of trade under the antitrust laws.

Addressing itself to the deeply vexatious issue of labor injunctions, section 20, in superbly ambiguous language, declared that no restraining order be issued by federal courts "unless necessary to prevent irreparable injury to property, or to a property right." Samuel Gompers seized upon the rhetoric of the labor provisions in the statute and in a grandiose mood hailed its passage as "the Magna Carta upon which the working people will rear their struc-

---

[50] Kirk H. Porter and Donald Bruce Johnson, compilers, *National Party Platforms, 1840–1960* (Urbana: University of Illinois Press, 1961), p. 148.
[51] Arthur S. Link, *American Epoch: A History of the United States Since the 1890's* (New York: Alfred A. Knopf, 1956), pp. 66–67.

ture of industrial freedom." [52] But many newspaper editorials, politicians, and even some labor spokesmen opined that the Clayton Act's cautious phraseology did not suddenly vest labor with any new rights, nor had the injunction been outlawed.[53] But lay opinion is extraneous; in the final analysis it is the Supreme Court which authoritatively determines congressional intent.

An early harbinger of future legal interpretation came from former President and future Chief Justice (1921–30) William Howard Taft. Taft in October 1914, in his presidential address to the American Bar Association, expressed the view that sections 6 and 20 were but "declaratory merely of what would be the law without the statute." [54] During Taft's first year as Chief Justice, in 1921, his previously expressed private view that the common-law conspiracy doctrine simply had been statutorily reinforced was reiterated almost identically by the Supreme Court, which now made officially clear the relative unimportance to labor of the Clayton Act; it was "merely declaratory of what was the best practice always." [55]

Although the declaration in section 6 that labor was not a commodity remained, it had no immediate practical effects on labor-management relations, and little, if any, weight with the courts. Its significance was that it marked a change in general public attitudes toward unionization. But "the use of the anti-trust laws against labor," notes Bernstein, "reached a climax in the decade 1919–1929." During the twenties there were no fewer than twenty-three criminal prosecutions, six damage suits, and forty injunction suits. Gompers' belief in union exemption from judicial scrutiny was rudely jarred by a series of antilabor Supreme Court holdings. First the Court established antitrust jurisdiction over trade union activities, then it read picketing out of the protection of section 20, and in a momentous decision reasoned that if a union, striking to organize an unorganized segment of the industry, obstructed production, it would have an effect on commerce and violate the antitrust laws. And ultimately, the Court, for the first time, held a collective bargaining agreement illegal under the Sherman Act.[56]

[52] Bernstein, *op. cit.*, p. 208.
[53] Dulles, *op. cit.*, p. 204.
[54] Bernstein, *op. cit.*, p. 209.
[55] Fainsod, *op. cit.*, p. 176.
[56] Bernstein, *op. cit.*, p. 211.

While these adverse judicial decisions were both reflective and symptomatic of labor's lean years, other factors also contributed to the temporary decline and paralysis of the labor movement during the twenties. An anti-union drive, revived in 1919, received impetus and cohesion in January 1921, when, at a Chicago conference of state manufacturers' associations, the "American Plan" (a term so evocative of the postwar nationalism) became the cornerstone of business' counterattack. The American Plan, a euphemism for the open shop, implied more than the employer's right to hire non-union personnel; in actual practice it meant discrimination against union members and a refusal to recognize unions. The open shop movement, writes Dulles, became "a recognized technique for denying the whole process of collective bargaining in the relations between employer and employee." [57] The American Plan personified the contemporary ethos; it stressed the traditional and accepted values of individualism and implied that collective bargaining not only hampered personal self-advancement, but was subversive and "unAmerican." The soft sell of the "American Plan" was reinforced by coercive, intimidatory tactics. Some employers resorted to the use of labor spies, discriminatory hiring practices and black lists, strong-arm strikebreakers, and yellow-dog contracts.

The yellow-dog contract, a logical institutionalization of discriminatory hiring practices, is a written agreement signed by a worker as a condition of employment not to belong to a union and not to engage in certain specified activities, such as collective bargaining or striking. Essentially, this type of contract, called "individual" by the employer, is a form of pressure only slightly different from outright "union busting." The yellow-dog contract, originally prominent in the New England textile industry in the 1870's, gained a new notoriety a half-century later.

While the dramatic and easily identifiable forces of the prevalent social climate, such as court decisions and management actions, were important, other forces, much less dramatic and certainly much less easily discernible, especially while they were occurring, also contributed to labor blight during the period. Among these factors were: heterogeneous labor force — the older skilled, white labor population found little in common with the waves of

[57] Dulles, *op. cit.*, p. 246.

eastern and southern European immigrants who had come before the war and the quotas and who now swelled the working ranks; and the displaced farmer brought with him to the city the rural tradition of individualism. Economic expansion – the developing new industries, automobiles, chemicals, utilities, and rubber were anti-union, while older industries, steel, baking, and glass, merged and formed combinations hostile to collective bargaining. Migration of industry – industries relocated in areas where unionism was ineffectual or unestablished. And, finally, the unions themselves – craft unions were unable to make structural adaptations to include the rapid expansion of employment in service and distributive industries.[58]

Furthermore, some impulses toward unionism were deflected by management's initiation of "welfare capitalism." Welfare capitalism, called by its critics paternalism designed to avoid trade unionism, nonetheless improved work conditions, attempted to minimize the harsh hazards of an industrial society, and, most significantly, publicized and elevated the just needs and desires of the American laborer. But welfare capitalism did not reduce the management-union tensions in the sick coal and textile industries. Discussing these two industries during the decade 1920–30, historian Arthur S. Link has written:

Textiles and coal mining remained highly competitive, unstable, and plagued by overproduction and dislocations resulting from the movement of these industries into the low wage area of the South. To a large degree frontier social conditions still prevailed in mining areas and mill towns. Low wages and attempts by employers to preserve an industrial absolutism stimulated efforts at unionization; in turn these organizational campaigns were accompanied by the kind of violent warfare that had been often characteristic of the American industrial scene before the First World War.[59]

The uneven prosperity of the twenties, recorded in the stark farm figures, was also recorded in union statistics. Union membership of 5,047,800 in 1920 plummeted to 3,622,000 in 1923, and slowly declined to 3,442,000 in 1929.[60] Against this background of union atrophy, the Norris-LaGuardia Act took shape.

On December 12, 1927, as a favor to his friend Andrew Furuseth,

[58] Bernstein, *op. cit.*, pp. 87–89.
[59] Link, *American Epoch, op. cit.*, p. 348.
[60] Bernstein, *op. cit.*, p. 84.

president of the International Seaman's Union, Senator Henrik Shipstead of Minnesota introduced S.1482, which was referred to the Senate Judiciary Committee, chaired by George W. Norris. Drafted by salty, self-educated Furuseth, chief sponsor of the 1915 Seaman's Act, S.1482 attempted to free labor from the injunctive prohibitions by statutorily redefining the scope of injunctive relief. Norris chose Senators Tom Walsh of Montana and John J. Blaine of Wisconsin to join him as a subcommittee. From February 8 to March 22, 1928, the subcommittee considered the Shipstead bill but reluctantly came to the conclusion that Furuseth's proposal was inadequate. That May, Norris called in expert legal advisers, labor lawyer Donald Richberg, Professors Felix Frankfurter and Francis B. Sayre of Harvard, Joseph P. Chamberlain and Herman Oliphant of Columbia, to draft a more comprehensive bill. The new subcommittee bill, now known as the Norris bill, was accepted by the full Judiciary Committee; no further action was taken, however, because the Seventieth Congress adjourned for the 1928 presidential campaign.

Senator Norris was even less successful in the Seventy-first Congress; there his anti-injunction bill was first reported adversely by the conservative-dominated Judiciary Committee and then pigeonholed. But the pigeonholing was only a temporary setback; the tide already had begun to favor the Nebraskan's position. Just prior to the unfavorable Judiciary Committee action, President Hoover nominated circuit court Judge John J. Parker to the Supreme Court. The nomination provoked an immediate storm of protest, for Parker had achieved considerable notoriety in his 1927 Red Jacket decision sanctioning yellow-dog contracts. Norris, with labor's blessing and support, mounted such a formidable attack on Parker's elevation that for the first time in thirty-six years an appointment to the High Court was rejected by the Senate. The controversy over Parker's appointment, however, important as it was, transcended the issue of his nomination and served to publicize labor's ever-growing grievances with the judiciary.

As a result of increasing public awareness, labor's anti-injunction movement began to receive broad-based support. In late 1930, the American Civil Liberties Union sponsored the formation of the National Committee on Labor Injunctions which dedicated itself to the support of the Norris bill. Additional support came in

January 1931 when the National Civic Federation's commission on industrial inquiry also announced its support of the Norris bill. In February 1931 the National Committee on Labor Injunctions made public a model state anti-injunction bill based on the Norris measure. That July, in a pioneering step, Wisconsin enacted a "little Norris-LaGuardia Act" characterized by *The Nation* as "the most progressive piece of labor legislation in the country." [61] Other legislation protecting labor was enacted in New York, Pennsylvania, Ohio, Oregon, and Colorado, preparing the way for the passage of the Norris-LaGuardia Anti-Injunction Act of 1932.

On January 27, 1932, the Senate Judiciary Committee reported the bill favorably, and, on February 23, Norris presented the bill to the Senate. In arguing for his bill, the Nebraskan maintained that the writ of injunction, an extraordinarily harsh remedy, "should never be resorted to except in cases where irreparable injury will result." The real object of the injunction was not "to protect property but to restrain the constitutional rights of individuals and thus to interfere with human liberty." [62] Senator Norris linked injunctions with the growth of immense concentrations of wealth and capital. As monopoly increased its hold on business undertakings, the use of the injunction in labor disputes proliferated. It was unfair for the ordinary laboring man to be forced to cope with these monolithic giants of capital without the full benefits and techniques associated with unionism. Norris summed up his philosophy of labor relations by declaring:

Laboring men have organized into associations and unions in order that they may present a united front to the demands of combined wealth and great aggregations of capital. His [*sic*] right to do this has become universally recognized, but, by means of harsh, cruel, and misused injunctive process, monopoly, through the assistance of our courts, has interfered by means of injunctions, which in their effect, have often taken away the real right of labor to have a voice in the wage it shall receive, and the effect has often been involuntary servitude on the part of those who must toil in order that they and their families may live. Such conditions bring about involuntary servitude — a species of economic slavery — which cannot permanently exist in a free country. . . . The man who by force of economic conditions, is compelled to toil against his wish and under conditions depriving him of his freedom, is a slave.[63]

[61] Quoted in *ibid.*, p. 411.
[62] *Cong. Record*, 72d Cong., 1st sess. (February 23, 1932), Vol. 75, pt. 4, p. 4502.
[63] *Ibid.*

The Nebraskan was particularly angered by the fact that many of the injunctions issued by the courts in labor disputes were based on yellow-dog contracts. He recognized that it was the legal effect of the yellow-dog contract which gave it its importance, and he believed it sound public policy to outlaw it as a basis for the granting of legal or equitable relief by any United States court. In urging the outlawing of the yellow-dog contract, the Senator argued that on the basis of common law such contracts, instead of being enforced, ought to have been declared null and void. He advanced three reasons for this position. First, the yellow-dog contract was contrary to public policy under the common law because "if men must agree in advance to surrender any liberty of contract in order to obtain employment, they are under coercion of necessity forced into working under conditions of involuntary servitude." Second, yellow-dog contracts should have been held void because they were entered into without consideration. In such a contract the employer surrendered none of his freedom of action and furnished "no consideration from the promise of the employee that he will surrender his ordinary rights of liberty of contract which are inherent in every free citizen." Third, yellow-dog contracts were invalid to begin with because they were signed under duress and coercion, the employee being forced to accept all of the burdensome and unreasonable conditions imposed upon him in order to support his family.[64]

Norris' arguments were seconded by Senators Blaine, Walsh, and Wagner, and on March 1, 1932, the Senate overwhelmingly passed the Norris bill 75 to 5. In the House, fiery New York Congressman Fiorello H. LaGuardia who "had no prior connection with anti-injunction legislation," introduced the bill and thereby attached his name to the legislation. House debate on the bill was desultory, but momentarily brightened somewhat when rabidly conservative Pennsylvania Republican James Beck, former Solicitor General under Harding, shrilly predicted that enactment of the bill would be "a long march toward Moscow." Beck's was a lonely voice, however. The House, voting 362 to 14, firmly approved.[65]

[64] *Cong. Record*, 72d Cong., 1st sess. (February 23, 1932), Vol. 75, pt. 4, p. 4504.
[65] Bernstein, *op. cit.*, p. 413.

The overwhelming endorsement in both the Senate and the House made it politically unwise for Hoover to veto the Act. But when the President signed the Norris-LaGuardia Act on March 23, 1932, he attempted to neutralize his approval by releasing at the same time an opinion by Attorney General Mitchell. Mitchell's statement declared that the bill, being controversial, would be subject to judicial decision, but it appeared that antitrust suits to enjoin conspiracies would still be permissible. Norris, incensed by the White House's calculated issuance of the memorandum, immediately fired back a burning retort in which the opinion was characterized as a device by which corporations would litigate in the hope of invalidating the statute. Enactment of this legislation and President Hoover's very reluctant signing of it may partially be explained by the awareness on the part of both major political parties that the approaching election would be held under conditions of extreme economic stress.

The Norris-LaGuardia Anti-Injunction Act of 1932 attempted to free labor from the restrictions imposed by previous legislation and establish a declaration of public policy "to assist the courts in the proper interpretation of the proposed legislation." Norris correctly believed the declaration to be "the first time in the history of the United States that any attempt has been made to declare, through an act of Congress, the public policy of the United States in relation to the issuing of injunctions in labor controversies." [66] The extraordinary section 2 of the Act states:

Under the prevailing economic conditions, developed with the aid of governmental authority for owners of property to organize in the corporate and other forms of ownership association, the individual unorganized worker is commonly helpless to exercise actual liberty of contract and to protect his freedom of labor, and thereby to obtain acceptable terms and conditions of employment, wherefore, although he should be free to decline to associate with his fellows, it is necessary that he have full freedom of association, self-organization and designation of representatives of his own choosing, and that he shall be free from the interference, restraint, or coercion of employers of labor, or their agents in the designation of such representatives or in self-organization or in other concerted activities for the purpose of collective bargaining or other mutual aid or protection.

[66] *Cong. Record*, 72d Cong., 1st sess. (February 23, 1932), Vol. 75, pt. 4, p. 4503.

The Norris-LaGuardia Act, in short, was based on the assumption that there ordinarily could be no equality of liberty of contract between employer and employee except on the basis of organized and collective bargaining. Norris believed that labor was at a distinct competitive disadvantage in relation to capital and that it was unable by itself to achieve fair and equitable working conditions without some form of federal supervision. However, in contrast with later more paternalistic New Deal labor legislation, the Norris-LaGuardia Act was primarily self-help legislation, in that it granted unions freedom from injunctive interference when pursuing their normal goals. While not completely forbidding the issuance of injunctions, judicial interdiction against normal union activities was prohibited since the substantive grounds for the issuance of labor injunctions were circumscribed in three respects: (1) Yellow-dog contracts, although still legal, were made unenforceable in the federal courts; (2) Injunctions under the antitrust laws might no longer be more extensive than those based on the common law; (3) In no case might a federal injunction prohibit certain normal labor practices (such as refusal to work, joining or remaining in a union, giving financial aid to a union or strikers, picketing or otherwise publicizing a labor dispute, assembling peaceably to promote their side of a dispute, etc.) when performed by persons either singly or in concert while participating in a labor dispute. Since the Act applies only when a labor dispute is found to exist, that term was defined in the broadest possible language.

Furthermore, additional procedural limitations were erected against the use of the labor injunction. Temporary or permanent injunctions might be issued only after the open hearing of witnesses in support of the complaint, subject to cross-examination, and after formal court determination of potential substantial and irreparable injury. Labor was greatly aided by the provisions that union officers or members, and the unions themselves, were liable for unlawful acts of individual members only "upon clear proof of actual participation in, or actual authorization of such acts." [67] The Act basically was negative legislation; it was limited to the important special purpose of ending judicial regulation of labor

[67] Fainsod, *op. cit.*, p. 180.

pressure against capital. It left the employer free to combat and to retaliate against union action.

Despite its importance, little contemporary attention was given to the enactment of the Norris-LaGuardia Anti-Injunction Act; nonetheless, its passage indicated a significant change in Congress' attitude toward the problems of unionism and industrial relations.

Writing in 1946, University of Chicago law professor Charles O. Gregory, a leading labor authority, noted in *Labor and the Law* that it is often claimed, with a good deal of justice, that the Federal Anti-Injunction Act is "the most revolutionary piece of labor legislation ever adopted by Congress, even including the later New Deal statutes." [68] It is significant that the National Industrial Recovery Act of 1933, a New Deal expedient designed to relieve the profound economic distress, was the first law that guaranteed to all workers the right to organize, yet much of the language of controversial section 7(a) of the NIRA, which gave this right to labor, was lifted bodily from the declaration of policy contained in the Norris-LaGuardia Act of 1932.

Although both the Mitchell opinion and existing court statements were an open invitation to question the constitutionality of the Norris-LaGuardia Act, it encountered no immediate judicial challenge. This anomaly ultimately was put to rest six years after the passage of the Act, when, in two cases decided that year, the Act was sustained. By 1947, sixteen states covering many of the important industrial areas of the United States had copied the anti-injunction provisions of the 1932 legislation and passed statutes modeled on the Norris-LaGuardia Act.[69]

Norris, as the Anti-Injunction Act indicates, was always on the side of the little man who was unable to protect himself from the predatory forces of society. During the Depression the Senator reasoned that it was better for the federal government to give a man a job than to permit him to remain idle, when he did not want to be idle, and had not caused his own unemployment. Government subsidization of the unemployed restored the individual's self-respect and dignity; it gave to the worker "an independence that cannot be his if he is compelled to receive charity to keep himself and his family alive." Norris wanted the Senate to declare

[68] Gregory, *op. cit.*, p. 191.
[69] Fainsod, *op. cit.*, p. 180.

war on unemployment and depression by adopting the extensive anti-depression legislation suggested by the 1932 Detroit Conference of Municipal Executives. When the Roosevelt administration came into office and urged upon Congress stopgap legislation to remedy the distressed condition of labor, Norris unstintingly gave his support. He was interested in people, not dollars, and did not concern himself with the niceties of self-liquidating projects as opposed to non-self-liquidating projects.[70]

The Nebraskan's concern for people had been recognized by leaders in the movement for labor progress long before the fight for anti-injunction legislation and the crisis of the Depression. After Senator La Follette died, Donald R. Richberg, at that time a militant progressive, approached Norris with worthwhile legislation for the protection of child laborers. The Senator, however, declined to introduce and fight for this particular labor advance because at that time he was too involved in the problems of Muscle Shoals.[71] This disinclination to introduce Richberg's proposal in no way reflected the Senator's feelings on the subject of child labor. He pragmatically recognized that

one reason why a Federal Law ought to be passed on the subject is because the States cannot, under existing conditions, get a uniform law. The result is that those who desire to employ child labor have better opportunities in some States than in others, and the tendency is for States, in order to get industries within their borders, to give advantage along such lines to manufacturing concerns. That makes it important to have a general law so there will be no discrepancies.

He always was exceedingly bitter about "the various corporations and concerns backed by many millions of capital, who want to make money out of the toil of little children" and consequently strenuously supported the Child Labor Amendment along with other legislation designed to ameliorate the onerous working conditions of women and children.[72]

When violence and bloodshed erupted in 1931 as a result of the unrelenting bitterness between the miners and the operators in the soft-coal fields of Harlan County, Kentucky, Theodore Dreiser, chairman of the National Committee for the Defense of Po-

[70] *Cong. Record*, 72d Cong., 1st sess. (June 18, 1932), Vol. 75, pt. 12, pp. 13350–52.
[71] Norris to Donald Richberg, July 18, 1925, Norris Papers.
[72] Norris to J. D. Ream, December 31, 1924, Norris Papers.

litical Prisoners, wrote to Norris and suggested that a resolution to investigate the situation in "bloody Harlan County" be introduced in the Senate. The Senator immediately replied that he had "no hesitancy whatever about introducing the resolution" and expressed his desire to aid the striking miners in any way possible.[73] Norris' concern can be attributed in part to his chance meeting with a miner who had been severely injured in a coal mine explosion. The incident had made such an impression on Norris that, in his Autobiography, he recalled that it lived in his memory throughout his life and aroused a "flood tide of emotion [which] had much to do" with his agitation for the passage of the anti-injunction legislation which bears his name.[74]

Yet although Senator Norris sympathized with labor and its cause, he did not permit his pro-labor feelings to dull his sense of justice. He adamantly refused, for example, to accept the AFL version of anti-injunction legislation and he bitterly opposed the sit-down strike as being "an illegal way of seeking redress on the part of labor." [75] He also opposed the labor-union practice of charging exorbitant admission fees as a prerequisite for employment in union shops. During the last months before World War II, he wrote to William Green, then president of the American Federation of Labor, that this practice of charging excessive union membership fees, particularly in instances of work on government projects, should be curtailed immediately. He was so vehement in his letter to Green that he threatened that if labor did not stop charging high membership fees it might become necessary for "Congress to have to pass legislation in regard to this which may be injurious to labor's cause." [76]

When belligerent, bushy-eyebrowed John L. Lewis led the Union Mine Workers of America out on strike in wartime, Norris was vitriolic in his condemnation of labor's antisocial attitude. In his Autobiography he commented caustically, "No man should strike against his country in time of war. No man, representing either management or labor, should resort to strike methods in

---

[73] Norris to Theodore Dreiser, October 29, 1931, Norris Papers.
[74] Norris, *Fighting Liberal, op. cit.,* p. 243.
[75] *Cong. Record,* 76th Cong., 1st sess. (June 12, 1939), Vol. 84, pt. 13, Appendix, p. 2529.
[76] Norris to William Green, reprinted in Washington *Daily News,* March 24, 1941, 16:4.

order to enforce demands in time of deadly peril. It seems to me
that the miners have forgotten the blessings and the rights given
them by the anti-injunction law, and have followed false leaders
who care more for their own ambitions than they do for freedom
and civilization in the world." [77] Norris' basic attitude toward labor
was sympathetic, nonetheless. He envisioned a six-hour work day
for the laborer. With his additional leisure time, the worker could
devote himself to worthwhile self-cultivation and enjoyment. He
realized that unremitting toil, without sufficient surcease, was destructive of human dignity.[78]

While Senator Norris' interest in agricultural problems can perhaps be explained in terms of his background and his constituency,
these things do not explain his abiding concern for labor. Norris'
genuine sympathy for, and his concerted interest in, the worker's
problems, though seemingly unusual in a senator who represented
predominantly rural Nebraska, had roots much deeper, and much
less complicated, than the heritage of midwestern farmer-labor
politics. In fact, as with so many other things Norris did, his espousal of labor's cause had an ethical rather than a political basis.
His sympathy with labor was a natural outgrowth of his feeling
that immense combinations of capital and monopoly were op-
pressing labor for their own venal ends. Both the worker and the
farmer were being squeezed by the plutocrats; both were depressed. Labor, as a depressed segment of the population, was
entitled to governmental protection to help place it in a position of
competitive equality with capital.

Senator Norris insisted that his anti-injunction legislation was
nothing more than statutory recognition of elemental justice. The
Norris-LaGuardia Act "gave labor," he subsequently reflected in
his Autobiography, "no right that any American citizen ought not
to possess in his daily life and in his day in court." It was the application of "the same rule of law to the poor as to the rich; to the
ignorant as well as the wise; to the weak as well as to the strong." [79]
His major legislative achievement on behalf of labor, the Federal

[77] Norris, *Fighting Liberal, op. cit.*, p. 316.
[78] George W. Norris, "Address at the University of Illinois on Receiving the
Cardinal Newman Award," November 16, 1933, reprinted in *Cong. Record*,
73d Cong., 2d sess. (January 12, 1934), Vol. 78, pt. 1, p. 521.
[79] Norris, *Fighting Liberal, op. cit.*, p. 317. *Cong. Record*, 72d Cong., 1st sess.
(February 23, 1932), Vol. 75, pt. 4, p. 4509.

Anti-Injunction Act, represented a gigantic step in the progress of the labor movement toward recognition and self-sufficiency. But Norris was not content to champion the cause of particular groups in the economy. Of all his struggles in Congress, perhaps he is best known for his advocacy of the rights of all the people in the fight for the preservation and development of America's natural resources.

NATURAL RESOURCES

George W. Norris always believed in and fought for the classic conception of conservation: "the use of the natural resources for the greatest good of the greatest number for the longest time." [80] With simple religious fervor the Senator moralized that, since natural resources were given "by an all-wise Creator to his people," it was merely just that "the development and conservation of these resources ought always to be under the public control, public ownership, and public operation." [81] No man or organization had the right to hinder their fullest development.

Norris recognized that the balance of nature has a direct relationship to modern technology and industrial needs. Accordingly, he approached the problem of conservation from the viewpoint of multipurpose development of natural regions, involving soil conservation, reforestation, irrigation, flood control, and navigation, as well as the production of electrical energy and power. In his Autobiography he commented, "From the beginning to the end, there was that irreconcilable conflict between those who believed the natural wealth of the United States can best be developed by private capital and enterprise, and those who believe

[80] Samuel P. Hays's provocative interpretation of the conservation movement rejects the traditional struggle thesis and propounds the theory that "conservation, above all, was a scientific movement, and its role in history arises from the implications of science and technology in modern society. . . . It is from the vantage point of applied science, rather than of democratic protest, that one must understand the historic role of the conservation movement." See: Samuel P. Hays, *Conservation and the Gospel of Efficiency: The Progressive Conservation Movement, 1890–1920* (Cambridge: Harvard University Press, 1959), p. 2. David Cushman Coyle, *Conservation* (New Brunswick: Rutgers University Press, 1957), p. vii. This definition has been ascribed to W. J. McGee.
[81] Norris, *Fighting Liberal, op. cit.*, p. 161.

that in certain activities related to the natural resources only the great strength of the Federal government itself can perform the most necessary task in the spirit of unselfishness, for the greatest good to the greatest number." [82]

The proving ground of Norris' vision was the Tennessee Valley Authority, perhaps his greatest claim to lasting renown. The TVA has "not only enabled more than a million and a third people in seven states to rehabilitate their farms, their lives, and their communities, but has demonstrated to the world that such methods are practicable and economically sound." [83] The TVA, for Norris and millions of others, represented American democracy at work. It was based on a broad construction of the Constitution and the recasting of federalism along natural regional lines. It involved large-scale social planning, new techniques of administration, and the alliance of science and politics. The TVA was initiated frankly as an experiment and administered in "the spirit of exploration and innovation." [84]

But before "the dreamers with shovels" had turned the first spadeful of earth in the Tennessee Valley, a bitter and protracted struggle had ensued between the conservationists, who believed in the public development and operation of natural resources, and the laissez-faireists, who advocated uninhibited private enterprise. Norris first became involved as a member of the House of Representatives. On February 23, 1911, the House was discussing a bill which would have given, without any restrictions, part of the public domain to the city of Seattle, Washington, for the purpose of expanding and improving the city's water supply. Representative Norris opposed the blanket disposal of public lands and predicted that the cession of land to a municipality "would establish a precedent . . . [Congress] will meet it time and time again in the future when individuals and corporations will be asking for some of the public domain." [85] Suggesting a change in the government's policy of land disposal, he recommended that, rather

[82] *Ibid.*, p. 246.
[83] Obituary, "Senator George W. Norris," *Commonweal*, XL (September 15, 1944), 508.
[84] David E. Lilienthal, *TVA: Democracy on the March* (New York: Harper and Brothers, 1944), p. 6.
[85] *Cong. Record*, 61st Cong., 3d sess. (February 23, 1911), Vol. 46, pt. 4, p. 3182.

than give lands away without any limitation, Congress should provide that the land could not be alienated by the donee, or used for
purposes other than those indicated by the grant, without the consent of Congress. In this instance the Nebraskan was concerned
that there might be mineral deposits on the lands which would be
ceded to Seattle. He feared that it would not be the city which
received the minerals, but some powerful interest which might
eventually exploit them.[86]

It was not until Norris reached the Senate, however, that he
developed a philosophy regarding the usage of natural resources
and water-power generation. His position first emerged during
the discussion of the Hetch Hetchy Act of 1913 (Raker Act). At
that time Norris was a member of the Senate Committee on
Public Lands which conducted hearings on the bill.

The bill, introduced by Representative John E. Raker, Democrat of California, authorized the city of San Francisco to develop
a reservoir site in the Hetch Hetchy Valley near Yosemite National Park and allowed the development of a municipally owned
hydroelectric power system. A section was added to the bill
which required the city to distribute the electric power to the
ultimate consumers and expressly forbade the disposition of it
wholesale to any individual or private utility under penalty of
forfeiture of the grant. This section was the most controversial of
the bill and made Hetch Hetchy a national issue.[87] Senator Norris
vigorously supported the bill and charged that the private utilities
were duping nature lovers into opposing the bill:

Pass this bill and you relieve the burden of every man on that [Pacific]
coast who earns his living by the sweat of his face. . . . pass this bill
and you will perform the highest act of conservation. Conservation does
not mean to lock up resources. Conservation does not mean dealing
out these resources to private capital for gain . . . here will be an
instance where the cheapest power on earth will be developed and
where it will be sold at cost. Defeat this bill and you will get the plaudits
and praises of every hydro-electric company in California. Pass it and

[86] *Ibid.*, p. 3183.
[87] Judson King, *The Conservation Fight: From Theodore Roosevelt to the
Tennessee Valley Authority* (Washington, D. C.: Public Affairs Press, 1959),
p. 42. Norris devotes an entire chapter of his Autobiography to Hetch Hetchy
and comments that "Hetch Hetchy is worthy of examination for the light it
sheds on the exact character of a fight which has been in progress for years."
Norris, *Fighting Liberal, op. cit.*, p. 162.

you put into the hands of the people a power God intended should do some good to man.[88]

The battle lines, formed during the Hetch Hetchy fight, were carried over into the debate on the Shields General Leasing bill of 1916. Senator John K. Shields, Democrat of Tennessee, had introduced a measure which would have shaped governmental conservation and water-power policy in a way which had the warm approval of the private utilities. Norris, aware of this, warned that valuable resources were being given away without any provision for safeguarding the interests of the public, and introduced a number of amendments designed to strengthen federal control. One amendment would have placed the issuing of leases in the hands of Congress, another would have increased the rental to be paid to the national government, and still another provided that corporations might exercise the right to eminent domain only in state courts.[89] Along with these amendments, a rider introduced by Norris, which called for the construction of a government-owned power project on the Great Falls of the Potomac River, was rejected by the Senate.[90] The Senator had hoped to develop power at the Great Falls, "not only for the benefit of the Government and the people of Washington, D.C., but also as an object lesson for the entire country."[91]

However, Norris' battle for conservation, multipurpose river development, and public generation of electric power had just begun. For over a decade, until the establishment of the TVA, the Nebraskan was the central figure in the struggle over private versus public disposition and usage of Muscle Shoals.

Muscle Shoals, a series of whirlpools and rapids on the Tennessee River, is a natural source of water power. This was recognized as early as 1899 when Congress granted a franchise for its development to the Muscle Shoals Hydro-Electric Company. But the franchise lapsed because of a dispute between Alabama and the federal government as to whom the company should pay for the privilege of developing the Shoals. President Theodore Roose-

[88] *Cong. Record*, 63d Cong., 2d sess. (December 6, 1913), Vol. 51, pt. 1, p. 347.
[89] *Ibid.*, 64th Cong., 1st sess. (February 23, 1916), Vol. 53, pt. 3, pp. 2966,. 2976.
[90] *Ibid.*, 64th Cong. 1st sess. (February 25, 1916), Vol. 53, pt. 4, p. 3140.
[91] *Ibid.*, 66th Cong., 2d sess. (January 14, 1920), Vol. 59, pt. 2, p. 1523.

velt vetoed similar franchises in 1903 and 1908.[92] In 1914 an Army Engineers' Survey reported that the area's mineral, forest, and agricultural resources were being wasted by the non-development of Muscle Shoals. President Wilson, acting under the authority of the National Defense Act of 1916, selected Muscle Shoals as a site on which the United States would construct a water-power development for the generation of electricity to be used in the manufacture of nitrates. Two nitrate plants were built and the construction of Wilson Dam was begun. After World War I, the Wadsworth-Kahn bill was introduced (November 1919), which provided that the plants be operated by a government-owned corporation which would use the electric power from Wilson Dam in the manufacture of commercial fertilizer. Surplus power, not used in the manufacture of nitrates, was to be sold. Although the bill passed the Senate on January 14, 1921, it was defeated in the House. The newly inaugurated Harding administration, in its effort to remove the government from business enterprises, stopped construction on Wilson Dam in April 1921, and attempted to liquidate its Muscle Shoals holdings.[93]

When industrialist Henry Ford submitted an offer, on July 8, 1921, to the War Department for the leasing of the Muscle Shoals property, it seemed very probable that the war-inspired government development would soon be under private control.[94] The Ford offer was initially rejected by Secretary of War John W. Weeks. But after much pro-Ford pressure Weeks reconsidered and submitted the Ford proposal along with comments which, in effect, recommended its rejection. In the Senate the Ford bid immediately became subject to a dispute over committee jurisdiction. The committee wrangle was resolved in favor of powerful Democrat Oscar W. Underwood of Alabama, one of the principal Ford supporters, who wanted the offer to go to the Agriculture Committee. This seemingly minor incident proved to be of major importance. It brought Muscle Shoals into the sphere of Committee Chairman Norris. At that time Norris was open-minded about

[92] Donald Floyd Danker, *Senator George W. Norris and Federal Water Power Legislation* (unpublished Master's thesis, University of Nebraska, 1949), p. 4.
[93] Preston J. Hubbard, *Origins of the TVA: The Muscle Shoals Controversy, 1920–1932* (Nashville: Vanderbilt University Press, 1961), pp. 5–27.
[94] C. Herman Pritchett, *The Tennessee Valley Authority: A Study in Public Administration* (Chapel Hill: University of North Carolina Press, 1943), p. 8.

the Ford plan. He observed, however, that the alternative of continued government operation of the Shoals had not been adequately considered.[95]

During the Senate hearings, in May 1922, Norris introduced his first Muscle Shoals bill. The Norris counter-proposal provided for government ownership of all Muscle Shoals property. The project, to be operated by the Federal Chemical Corporation, with a board of directors appointed by the President and confirmed by the Senate, was to make both explosives and fertilizer, and also to sell surplus power. The bill, in addition, authorized the Secretary of War to survey the Tennessee River in order to locate dams for storage reservoirs and possible power projects. Although Norris could not get the committee to recommend this bill, he did succeed in getting committee rejection of all private bids for Muscle Shoals.

Norris believed that the acceptance of the Ford offer, which he characterized as "the most wonderful real-estate speculation since Adam and Eve lost title to the Garden of Eden," would amount to an abandonment of wise conservation practices.[96] In the Senate and in numerous magazine articles, he repeatedly defended his stand against the popular Henry Ford. In *The Nation* he wrote that he "would not give away the heritage of the people even to a saint" and suggested that if Ford were in earnest about making cheap fertilizer he could obtain other water-power sites. In *The Saturday Evening Post* he reviewed the Ford offer and described the great mass of pressure being exerted on him. He noted a telegram received from a group of ministers, "The Muscle Shoals Holiness Association," who were pledged to pray that God might defeat all opposition to the Ford offer. Somewhat dryly, he observed that at least the Ford offer had been appealed to the highest possible authority.[97]

The enthusiasm for the Ford proposal extended to the Nebraska state legislature, which requested that all the state's congressmen support its passage so that a precedent could be set for a similar

[95] Hubbard, *op. cit.*, pp. 45–49. King, *op. cit.*, p. 109.
[96] Quoted in *ibid.*, pp. 76–77.
[97] George W. Norris, "Why Henry Ford Wants Muscle Shoals," *The Nation*, CXVII (December 26, 1923), 738. George W. Norris, "Shall We Give Muscle Shoals to Henry Ford?" *The Saturday Evening Post*, CXVI (May 31, 1924), 125.

development in Nebraska. Norris rather ironically replied that he was "unwilling to give away the birthright of millions of unborn citizens for the enrichment of private corporations . . . even when requested to do it by so high and honorable body as the House of Representatives of the Nebraska Legislature.[98]

While the Ford offer was still actively under consideration, the Teapot Dome oil scandal boiled over. Public indignation at this loot of natural resources was spontaneous. The progressives in Congress seized this opportunity to propose public ownership of natural resources in a measure introduced by Senator Norris and Representative Oscar E. Keller, independent Republican of Minnesota. The Norris-Keller bill, which was endorsed by the Public Ownership League of America, attempted to create a Federal Public Service Commission to cooperate with the states and municipalities in the development of a publicly owned and operated "superpower system" which would sell its service to the public at cost. The power system would, in addition, produce nitrates for fertilizer, also to be sold to farmers at cost. The Norris-Keller bill, however, died quietly.[99]

That same year, 1924, the Nebraskan introduced a revised version of his 1922 Muscle Shoals bill. His new bill reflected a more mature understanding of the interrelationship between conservation, natural resources, and power development. Instead of creating a Federal Chemical Corporation to manage the site, a Federal Power Corporation was to be created, and for the first time the government was authorized to construct high-tension transmission lines for the sale of power. Opposition by both Democrats and Republicans prevented passage of this bill during the session. "The issue of private versus public power was never very prominent nationally during this period of the controversy," writes Preston J. Hubbard, "and was completely overshadowed by the struggle between Ford and the power companies." [100]

In 1924 Ford withdrew his offer, and, in Norris' words, "the struggle over Muscle Shoals simplified itself to an issue between those who believed in public ownership and development of the

[98] *Cong. Record,* 67th Cong., 4th sess. (February 20, 1923), Vol. 64, pt. 4, p. 4056.
[99] *New York Times,* March 11, 1924, 11:7.
[100] Hubbard, *op. cit.,* p. 143.

power at Muscle Shoals and throughout the entire Tennessee Valley, and the 'power trust,' seeking to prevent everything of the kind." [101] The significance of Muscle Shoals transcended the colorful news copy written about Henry Ford, George Norris, and other notables of the period. It was now clear that Muscle Shoals was inextricably entangled in two of the most important postwar problems: water power and the protection of the public interest in government-owned natural resources.

Coolidge, on December 3, 1924, in a message to Congress, highlighted the still unresolved Muscle Shoals problem. Senator Underwood, with Administration backing, then attempted to resolve the issue. Underwood offered a new bill in the form of an amendment as a substitute to the 1924 Norris bill which was now before the Senate. The Underwood bill, a very limited solution, de-emphasized power production and emphasized the production of fertilizer. In the heated debate between the Administration-Underwood coalition and the Norris forces, the basic issue of public versus private operation of power utilities began to emerge. It was argued in support of the Underwood bill that agriculture and national defense would be best served by private operation of the Shoals. Senator Hefflin, summarizing the prevailing fear of government operation, called the Norris bill "socialistic" and "Bolshevistic." In rebuttal, the Norris bloc maintained that it was a legitimate governmental function to operate yardstick power projects as a means of regulating private power production. During the fray Norris unmercifully attacked Coolidge. While most of the Republicans remained silent, Underwood and Joseph T. Robinson of Arkansas defended the President. Ironically, Norris, a Republican, was taking his criticism, almost verbatim, from the Democratic literature of the 1924 presidential campaign, while the two southern Democrats were forced into the untenable position of having to defend the Republican President.

Although the Underwood bill passed the Senate, Norris twice succeeded in bottling up the conference report; at the close of the session no settlement on Muscle Shoals had been reached. After the fruitless debate on the Underwood bill, Coolidge, in response to a House resolution sponsored by Representative Martin B. Madden of Illinois, appointed a Muscle Shoals Commission of In-

---

[101] Norris, *Fighting Liberal, op. cit.,* p. 260.

quiry.[102] The Commission Report set off another round of controversy and on January 5, 1926, Norris again introduced a bill for the development of Muscle Shoals. This bill was even more comprehensive than its predecessors in that it called for multipurpose development of the watershed providing for maximum navigation, power, flood control, and the experimental production of fertilizer under the management of a government corporation. This proposal, after compromise in the Committee on Agriculture, passed the Senate but died in the House.[103] Some small measure of success was now apparent. Somewhat encouraged, early in the first session of the Seventieth Congress, on December 15, 1927, Norris introduced a modification of his earlier bills.

This new Norris proposal was designed to provide a temporary remedy for the situation at Muscle Shoals. The new bill did not provide for a comprehensive river development program, but it did allow the creation of a government corporation which would engage in fertilizer experimentation, production of fixed nitrogen, and the sale of surplus power.[104] The bill passed both Houses of Congress, and Norris, for the first time, nearly saw victory; but President Coolidge quietly gave it a pocket veto. Norris furiously issued a bitter statement denouncing Coolidge:

. . . The President with his keen, broad, New England foresight may be right in attempting to kill the bill without stating his objections to it in a veto message. . . . To have offended the Great Water Power Trust by approving of the Muscle Shoals Bill would have dried up sources of revenue that we must have in the campaign ahead of us. The veto may drive away from the Republican Candidate a large number of thinking citizens, but it will give us money in unlimited profusion and enable us to win the election by controlling the political machine and the sources of publicity.[105]

[102] Hubbard, *op. cit.*, pp. 148–75.
[103] King, *op. cit.*, p. 166.
[104] Pritchett, *The Tennessee Valley Authority, op. cit.*, p. 12.
[105] *New York Times*, June 9, 1928, 7:4. "Norris and LaGuardia challenged the legality of the Coolidge pocket veto. They interpreted that part of the United States Constitution which permits the President to void a bill in this manner as applying only to adjournments *sine die* and not to an *ad interim* adjournment as was the case in this instance. Many legal authorities felt that the Norris-LaGuardia contention possessed merit. Since the Okanogan Indians, whose claims had been embodied in a bill which also had received a pocket veto at this time, were carrying their case to the courts on this constitutional point, Norris held out hope that the Muscle Shoals bill would become law. But the United States Supreme Court, which finally handed down a decision on the

Despite the Coolidge pocket veto, Norris persevered. In an article for *Current History,* he reviewed the arguments in favor of the vetoed bill and declared that it would "have established a milestone in human progress." [106] Undaunted, he introduced another Muscle Shoals bill in the first session of the Seventy-first Congress, but it was not acted upon. In March 1930, he again introduced a bill similar to the one vetoed by Coolidge. Congressional passage of this bill, nearly a year later in a Democratic-controlled Congress, represented a personal victory for Norris.

But the battle was not yet won — presidential approval was needed. In a press statement on February 28, 1931, Hoover blandly said, "This happens to be an engineering project and so far as its business merits and demerits are concerned is subject to the cold examination of engineering facts. I am having these facts exhaustively determined by the different departments of the government and will then be able to state my views upon the problem." Norris' rebuttal was immediate. The next day, he acidly commented, "The great engineer is asking advice on an 'engineering project' from those who are not engineers, and when those who are not engineers tell the engineer what to do with 'an engineering project' the engineer will know whether to sign or veto the bill. It reminds me of the New England country justice who, at the close of a law suit, said he would take it under advisement for three days, at which time he would render judgment for the plaintiff." Not unexpectedly, on March 3, 1931, Hoover vetoed the Muscle Shoals bill.[107] The President, in a message which remains the classic epitome of bankrupt vision, attempted to justify his action:

. . . For the federal government deliberately to go out to build up and expand an occasion to the major purpose of a power and manufacturing business is to break down the initiative and enterprise of the American people; . . . it is the negation of the ideals upon which our civilization has been based. . . . I hesitate to contemplate the future of our institutions, of our country, if the preoccupation of its officials is to be no longer the promotion of justice and equal opportunity, but is to be

Okanogan Indian case in May 1929, held that the Coolidge pocket vetoes were legal." Hubbard, *op. cit.,* p. 235.
[106] George W. Norris, "Possibilities of the Completed Plant," *Current History,* XXVIII (August 1928), 733.
[107] Hubbard, *op. cit.,* p. 291.

devoted to barter in the markets. That is not liberalism, it is degeneration.

Norris, anguished and bitter at seeing his plans defeated a second time by presidential action, commented that Hoover had taken Muscle Shoals away from the people and had given it to the trusts by "his wicked, his cruel, his unjust, his unfair, and his unmerciful veto." [108]

The Hoover veto was the turning point in the Muscle Shoals controversy. It summarized the prevailing antipathy to government participation in the economy and forcefully enunciated the laissez-faire doctrine. The intellectual climate, however, was changing under the pressure of catastrophic economic events. When Franklin D. Roosevelt became President on March 4, 1933, a large proportion of the population was unemployed and business was at a standstill. Water power had been an issue in the 1932 campaign and a Depression-harassed public had become more sensitive to the charges that the "power trust" was abusing its monopoly position by charging high rates and refusing to undertake rural electrification. Consequently, FDR's acceptance of Norris' proposals was well received. In a message to Congress characterized by strong social vision, President Roosevelt stated:

. . . The continued idleness of a great national investment in the Tennessee Valley leads me to ask Congress for legislation necessary to enlist this project in the service of the people. It is clear that the Muscle Shoals development is but a small part of the potential public usefulness of the entire Tennessee River. Such use, if envisioned in its entirety, transcends mere power development; it enters the wide fields of flood control, soil erosion, afforestation, elimination from agricultural use of marginal lands, and distribution and diversification of industry. In short, this power development of war days leads logically to national planning for a complete watershed involving many States and the future lives and welfare of millions. It touches and gives life to all forms of human concerns.

I, therefore, suggest to the Congress legislation to create a Tennessee Valley Authority — a corporation clothed with the power of Government but possessed with the flexibility and initiative of a private enterprise. It should be charged with the broadest duty of planning for the proper use, conservation and development of the natural resources of the Tennessee River drainage basin and its adjoining territory for the general

[108] *Cong. Record*, 71st Cong., 3d sess. (March 3, 1931), Vol. 74, pt. 7, pp. 7047, 7084.

social and economic welfare of the Nation. . . . Many hard lessons have taught us the human waste that results from lack of planning. . . . It is time to extend planning to a wider field, in this instance comprehending in one great project many States directly concerned with the basin of one of our greatest rivers.[109]

A day after the President sent his message to Congress, Norris and Representative John J. McSwain, Democrat of South Carolina, simultaneously introduced bills in both the Senate and the House proposing the creation of the Tennessee Valley Authority. The next day the Senate Committee on Agriculture reported the Norris bill — in effect the bill which Hoover had vetoed — favorably. On May 18, 1933, FDR signed the Muscle Shoals bill and gave the pen to Norris. Aware of the significance of the creation of the TVA, the Nebraskan happily commented that "the Muscle Shoals legislation marks an epoch in the history of our national life. . . . It establishes a new governmental policy which if carried to its logical conclusion will bring blessing and comfort to our people." [110]

Senator Norris, however, was not content with the establishment of a single valley authority. He had believed for a long time that "it is a law of nature that one portion of the country can not permanently and properly and honestly be prosperous and happy while other great portions of the country are in distress and suffering from lack of the necessaries of life." [111] In line with this thinking he suggested that the TVA idea be carried forward in the form of enough valley authorities to cover the entire country. On June 3, 1937, he introduced a bill which divided the country into seven regional authorities patterned on the TVA. This proposal died in the Senate because of the problems and conflicting interests related to such matters as the reorganization of the executive branch of the government, strong opposition by the Corps of Army Engineers and by a considerable body of congressmen, and the hostility of established departments to any proposal to take away their own departmental powers and turn them over to a valley authority or similar agency.[112]

[109] Franklin D. Roosevelt, Address to Congress, April 10, 1933.
[110] *New York Times*, May 14, 1933, 2:1.
[111] *Cong. Record*, 70th Cong., 1st sess. (May 9, 1928), Vol. 69, pt. 8, p. 8186.
[112] William E. Leuchtenburg, "Roosevelt, Norris and the 'Seven Little TVA's,' " *Journal of Politics*, XIV (August 1952), 420.

The Senator, however, was more successful in his sponsorship of a measure to preserve America's forest lands. The Norris-Doxey Law of 1937 — backed by the Association of State Foresters and the American Forestry Association — expanded the technical advisory services to individual forest owners and encouraged tree planting. In arguing for this law, the Nebraskan pleaded that Congress leave to our country's children "an inheritance for our day, a duty well done." [113]

Norris' attitude toward conservation and natural resources was both practical and idealistic. He looked to the present as well as to the future. Perhaps of all the objectives for which he fought, the establishment of the Tennessee Valley Authority — with its associated controversy over Muscle Shoals — had the most enduring significance. The simple legend "Built for the People of the United States," which dedicates every TVA dam, has behind it a complexity of ideas which individually may not represent startling innovation, but which taken as an entity represent a gigantic forward step toward the realization that the federal government has a commitment to national planning and social engineering.

Nonetheless, not all the principles which Norris and the conservationists fought for have become settled policy. The cornerstone of the TVA philosophy is still subject to attrition by organized interests which cloak themselves in the symbols of states' rights and private enterprise. It still is not settled policy that the development of America's great river systems should be a coordinated multipurpose concern of the federal government. The champions of the "partnership principle" contest the fact that the most effective and economical way to control a river is to harness it and its tributaries, so as to create source-to-mouth usage which controls floods, erosion, and afforestation, prevents water pollution, and supplies adequate navigation and public power generation. In his Autobiography, Senator Norris prophetically warned that "there will never be a day that the American people can afford to be off guard. Only their vigilance will prevent misuse of the remaining resources of the nation." [114] This prediction

[113] *Cong. Record*, 75th Cong., 3d sess. (June 14, 1938), Vol. 83, pt. 8, p. 9205. For a technical discussion of this Act, see Ralph F. Wilcox, "Intensive Forestry Projects Under the Provisions of the Cooperative Farm Forestry Act," *Journal of Forestry*, XXXVIII (June 1940), 457–64.
[114] Norris, *Fighting Liberal, op. cit.*, p. 233.

has come to pass with the uproar over the Dixon-Yates deal and the shoddy application of the partnership principle to Hells Canyon. (The Hells Canyon case opened the way for the $200 million High Mountain Sheep Dam on the Snake River — a signal victory for private power interests over public power advocates.)[115]

But it is doubtful, even despite this opposition, that the principles embodied in the TVA will succumb to serious attenuation. It is now well over a quarter of a century since the Tennessee Valley Authority initiated its dramatic experiment in the use and control of a river for unified multipurpose development. Formerly an experiment, now an actuality, the TVA has proven extremely successful: the people of the Valley have had their per capita income rise dramatically; no damaging floods have swept the area since the storage system was completed; now pollution is controlled and the Tennessee is navigible for over 600 miles; the reforestry program has halted erosion and is producing wood; scores of dams have been built creating vast new sources of hydroelectric power harnessed for Valley electric requirements and omnipresent national defense needs. It is no wonder that the TVA is frequently cited as a viable example of democratic social engineering which is worthy of duplication and imitation in other countries.

The Nebraskan's dream of turning barren lands in the basin of the Tennessee River into productive valleys with renewed fertility is the epitome of his struggle for democracy. The TVA captures Norris' vision of a new America and symbolizes his hope that "if in the peaceful years ahead new vigor comes to old and wooden hills not only in the basin of the Tennessee but throughout America and in other regions of the world, and laughter replaces the silence of impoverished peoples, that is well." [116] Norris was a practical dreamer who had a positive vision of American democracy.

[115] The partnership principle was first announced by President Eisenhower in an address on September 23, 1954, at the dedication of the McNary Dam on the Columbia River. This principle, while approving comprehensive federal projects, nonetheless emphasizes that wherever possible private enterprise should be permitted to take over the power part of any project. Implicit in this is the recognition that private concerns should strive to meet the growing demands for power and that the federal government should retrench in the matter of power development and sales. See: King, *op. cit.*, p. 291. *New York Times*, February 6, 1964, 12:1.
[116] Norris, *Fighting Liberal, op. cit.*, p. 277.

☆　☆　☆　☆　☆　☆　☆　☆　☆

CHAPTER FIVE

Democracy and the World

☆　☆　☆　☆　☆　☆　☆　☆　☆

WAR: A RELIC OF BARBARISM

Although Norris was primarily interested in domestic reform, and made his greatest contributions to American democracy on the national scene, he was also very much aware of international events. The years from 1903 to 1942 in which he served in Congress marked the reluctant end of America's traditional policy of national-continentalism and saw the inchoate stages of a new foreign policy of internationalism. The United States, which had entered the twentieth century vigorously, triumphing over a declining Spain in a "splendid little war," was embroiled within two decades in a European war which was neither splendid nor little. World War I was followed by the Versailles Treaty, the League of Nations, a rejuvenated World Court, the pious Kellogg-Briand Pact, unfruitful disarmament conferences, and then by aggression and another world war. The turbulence of international affairs forced Norris to think about the problems of war and peace and to formulate a philosophy for the conduct of international affairs.

Of all the votes which Norris cast in his congressional career, perhaps he is best remembered for his vote against the United States' entrance into World War I. When President Woodrow

Wilson reluctantly presented to Congress his request that America "vindicate the principles of peace and justice"[1] so as to make the world safe for democracy, Senator Norris could not agree.

Two days after the President's address, on April 4, 1917, Norris arose in the Senate to oppose Wilson's request for a declaration of war. America's entrance into this foreign war, he orated, was not inspired by humanitarian considerations and would serve no cause of humanity. The United States was on the verge of war because "of the influence of money."[2] Norris contended that the American people had been tricked into a war hysteria by a large number of newspapers and news agencies in "the greatest propaganda that the world has ever known to manufacture sentiment in favor of war." America had been misled as "to the real history and true facts by the almost unanimous demand of the great combination of wealth that has a direct financial interest in our participation in the war." The Nebraskan further charged that the real reason the United States was entering the war was because Wall Street had "loaned many hundreds of millions of dollars to the Allies in this controversy."[3]

To support his views that financial involvement was a factor in causing America's entrance into the war, Norris quoted from a letter, written by a member of the New York Stock Exchange, which expressed "the Wall Street view" that stocks and bonds would appreciate when the United States entered the war. Carried away, the Senator gave hyperbolic expression to his devil theory of war. As anger seethed throughout the Senate chamber, the Nebraskan vehemently asserted:

War brings prosperity to the stock gamblers on Wall Street. To those who are already in possession of more wealth than can be realized or enjoyed. . . . Human suffering and the sacrifice of human life are necessary, but Wall Street considers only the dollars and cents . . . the stock brokers would not, of course, go to war, because the very object they have in bringing on war is profit, and therefore they must remain in their Wall Street offices in order to share in the great prosperity they say war will bring. The volunteer officer, even the drafting officer, will not find them. They will be concealed in their palatial offices on Wall Street, sitting behind mahogany desks, covered with clipped coupons—

[1] Woodrow Wilson, Address to Congress, April 2, 1917.
[2] U.S., *Congressional Record*, 65th Cong., 1st sess. (April 4, 1917), Vol. 55, pt. 1, p. 215.
[3] *Ibid.*, p. 213.

coupons soiled with the sweat of mothers' tears, coupons dyed in the lifeblood of their fellow man.

America was going into the war "upon the command of gold." A vote in favor of the war resolution was equivalent to committing a sin against humanity. Norris continued his diatribe, "I would like to say this to the war god: 'You shall not coin into gold the life-blood of my brethren'. . . . I feel we are about to put the dollar sign upon the American flag." The only reason America was entering the war was "to preserve the commercial right of American citizens to deliver munitions of war to belligerent nations." [4]

Senator Norris predicted that the munitions makers would make immense fortunes at the expense of society. Dire consequences might possibly follow. The balance of society would become poorer and poorer with the burden of increased taxation, until the country would in time become bankrupt, or else society would become bipolarized. Carried away by his own rhetoric he warned that there would be "a class of aristocracy and another class of citizens who would be practically slaves. All the property would be held by a few and in the end it would mean revolution." [5]

The argument outlining economic involvement was then buttressed by an appeal to traditional isolationist sentiments.[6] The troubles of Europe should be settled by Europe, the United States remaining absolutely neutral. He traced the route by which America had slowly retreated from neutrality to its current position on that unhappy April day. Both England and Germany had established military zones and warned neutral shipping not to enter the prohibited areas. In order to enforce their prohibitions, England had resorted to the use of submerged mines and Germany to the use of submarines. These actions on the part of the belligerents were contrary to all principles of international law and humanity. Germany was behaving with more humanity than England because the submarine was capable of exercising some degree of discretion and judgment, but the sea mine was an absolute unthinking menace to shipping.

[4] *Ibid.*, p. 214.
[5] *Cong. Record*, 64th Cong., 1st sess. (July 17, 1916), Vol. 53, pt. 11, p. 11189.
[6] Norris never changed his mind that the United States' entrance into World War I was motivated primarily by economics. Twenty years later, in a speech advocating President Franklin D. Roosevelt's cash and carry principle, he reaffirmed his belief that the dollar sign had been placed upon the American flag.

In elaborating on the consequences of the establishment of the war zones, Norris accused President Wilson of pro-British feeling. Of course, he reasoned, more ships and more American lives were lost from the action of submarines than from English mines in the North Sea simply because the Administration had acquiesced in the British zones and kept American ships out of it while we refused to recognize the legality of the German war zone. "The only difference between the two illegal military zones," stated Norris, "is that in the case of Germany we have persisted in our protest, while in the case of England we have submitted." [7]

Senator Norris postulated a series of four alternatives which the American government could have followed in the face of the extraordinary orders establishing war zones. First, America could have defied both England and Germany and gone to war with both these nations for violating international law and interfering with neutral rights. Second, America had a technical right to defy one and to acquiesce in the other. Third, America could have denounced their actions as illegal, acquiesced in them, and thus remained neutral with both sides. In short, this would have amounted to a declaration to American shipowners that these orders were unjust and contrary to international law, but the provocation was insufficient to cause the United States to go to war in defense of her neutral rights. Fourth, America might have declared an embargo against either belligerent which had persisted in maintaining its military zone. Norris was of the opinion that if America had followed this last alternative the zones would have been of short duration. America should have maintained from the beginning the strictest neutrality and would have avoided the present tragic circumstances. [8]

Not heeding the anti-war position of Norris, La Follette, and others, Congress declared war on Imperial Germany. Once America had joined the hostilities, Norris, notwithstanding his firm opposition to the war, supported the military program. He re-

[7] *Cong. Record*, 65th Cong., 1st sess. (April 4, 1917), Vol. 55, pt. 1, p. 214.
[8] Norris had previously offered an amendment to the ship purchase bill in the hope of maintaining neutrality. This amendment provided "that no vessel shall be purchased under this act which sails under the flag of any nation at war with any other nation which is at peace with the United States, unless prior to such purchase an understanding or agreement shall have been reached that will avoid any international difficulty or dispute regarding such purchase." *Ibid.*, 63d Cong., 3d sess. (January 29, 1915), Vol. 52, pt. 3, p. 2543.

mained convinced, however, that America had entered into an unholy crusade for unholy reasons.

Although morally opposed to war, Senator Norris was not a pacifist. During the middle 1930's, as a reaction to the harsh policies of militant dictatorships in Germany, Italy, and Japan, the Nebraskan began a slow intellectual transformation, his steadfast opposition to armament and American involvement in world affairs gradually wavering.[9]

By March 1938, after Hitler had occupied Austria and annexed it to Germany, Norris had come to believe that, unless the United States was prepared, developments outside American borders might invite war. He stated that he had modified his position somewhat "on the question of a large Navy at least to the extent" that America should be "armed to a greater extent than Japan is armed or greater than either Italy or Germany is armed." He had begun to realize that "if the policies of Hitler or Mussolini or Japan are carried to their logical conclusion the doctrine they advocate will spread and the civilized world ultimately will have to contend against the barbarous conduct they have inaugurated." "Force," he observed, "is the only thing which stops them from conquering the world." Six months before the Munich debacle signaled the impending European struggle, Senator Norris expressed a desire for United States participation in a conference with the other nations of the world opposed to the Rome-Berlin Axis. However, he was not in favor of any conference in which America would "be bound in any way to engage in war in Europe or Asia."[10] Armed neutrality should be the watchword for America.

Shortly after Hitler's armies invaded Poland, Norris, on October 3, 1939, delivered a nationwide radio address in which he outlined a policy for the American government to pursue which would be least liable to get America into another European war. He predicated his argument on the isolationist doctrine that "the struggle going on in Europe is Europe's struggle." It was a catastrophe which was beyond the jurisdiction of the United States. America should learn from the lessons of the last war. The United States

[9] The first indication that Norris was altering his preparedness position came after Mussolini's attack on Ethiopia. *Ibid.*, 74th Cong., 2d sess. (May 7, 1936), Vol. 80, pt. 6, p. 6805.
[10] *United States News*, March 28, 1938.

government, during World War I, had become a collection agency. "Financial influence was brought to bear to bring the American Government into the war." In order to prevent American blood again being coined into gold it was necessary to change the Embargo Law. Senator Norris followed President Roosevelt's foreign policy in urging a change in the neutrality legislation. He advocated the principle of cash and carry — it should be unlawful to export or transport to a belligerent nation anything of any kind until title to the property had been transferred and the goods paid for. "Therefore, no American citizen will have any interest whatever in the property sold, and if the property is destroyed on the seas, no American citizen will have any financial interest in it." The Nebraskan was in favor of making it unlawful for any American vessel to carry passengers or war materials to any port of a belligerent nation. In addition, no American citizen or vessel should be permitted to proceed into any combat area upon the seas. No American citizen should be permitted to travel on ships of any belligerent nation, and no commercial American ship should be armed. Norris favored FDR's proposal that it be made unlawful "for any person within the United States to purchase bonds or securities or other obligations of any belligerent government, or any political subdivision of such government." Neutrality would prevent Wall Street from pushing the United States into another war. In a letter to one of his correspondents, Norris reaffirmed his financial-interest theory of war. "If we continue to trade with warring nations, the danger will be that those who have thus obtained a financial interest in the war, will start propaganda in order to get America into the war to save their financial investments." [11]

Norris, in short, took the position that the prevention of economic ties and the elimination of possible incidents would prevent the United States from being catapulted into a European war. He conceded that the proposed changes in the Embargo Law — particularly the cash and carry principle — might be somewhat favorable to France and England. But France and England, after all, were fighting the battle for humanity and civilization against immoral and dishonorable foes.

Norris had slowly evolved a rationale which permitted him to

[11] George W. Norris, "American Neutrality," Radio Address, October 3, 1939, reprinted in *Cong. Record*, 76th Cong., 2d sess. (October 4, 1939), Vol. 85, pt. 2, Appendix, p. 128.

depart from his traditional isolationism, accepting a form of modified interventionism.[12] The Senator now believed that the "world is confronted with two radically different philosophies of government," democratic and dictatorial. The dictatorial philosophy of government — the Hitlerian ethic — had never before been proposed in any civilized society. "That theory is that any government has the right to conquer any other government or any other people if it has the power to do so."[13] This philosophy of government started first with Japan when she stole Manchukuo. Then Mussolini adopted the policy and conquered Abyssinia. Finally Hitler carried the precedent further, and Russia followed suit by making war on Finland.

By 1941, Norris had come to the conclusion that America must give aid as well as moral support to England in her battle against Hitler. Nevertheless, when the Lend-Lease bill, bearing the numerical designation H.R. 1776, a date so redolent of freedom, arrived in the Senate, Norris, despite his deep attachment to England's cause, could not completely abandon his strong isolationism. He proposed an amendment designed to insure against America's being drawn into a foreign war: "Nothing in this act shall be construed to authorize the President, without the consent of Congress, to send the armed forces of the United States to fight on foreign soil outside of the Western Hemisphere or the territorial or insular possessions of the United States, including the Philippine Islands."[14]

[12] Although Norris was willing to modify his previous stand against an increase in naval armament and support to the Allies, he nevertheless remained adamant in his opposition to compulsory military service. His great objection to such legislation was the effect it would have on America in the years to come. It would bring about a radical change in the historic course of the American nation — it would lead to militarism. "If we are to have compulsory military training in time of peace," he said in the Senate, "we shall put ourselves on a level with the dictator nations of the world." Compulsory military training, for Norris, was synonymous with militarism and all its evil effects. *Ibid.*, 76th Cong., 3d sess. (August 12, 1940), Vol. 86, pt. 9, p. 10113.
[13] This theory on forms of government and the need for American aid to England was set forth in Norris' radio address, "The Lend-Lease Bill," on February 26, 1941, and reached its climax in a commencement address given by him at Wooster College, Ohio, on June 16, 1941, in which the dictatorships were characterized as having "pagan philosophies of government." *Ibid.*, 77th Cong., 1st sess. (February 27, 1941), Vol. 87, pt. 10, Appendix, p. 873. *Ibid.* (June 16, 1941), Vol. 87, pt. 12, Appendix, p. 862.
[14] *Ibid.* (March 7, 1941), Vol. 87, pt. 2, p. 1979.

The Senator recognized that the passage of the Lend-Lease bill would convert the United States from a friendly neutral into a full-fledged non-belligerent. However, aside from the idealistic reasons for aiding Great Britain, he believed there were sound economic reasons for the lend-lease program. Should Hitler defeat England, he would then dominate Europe, shutting the United States out of European commerce. Hitler, moreover, would be able to infiltrate the South American countries. America would be confined to her own borders and her foreign trade would dwindle and finally disappear. Common business sense, Norris pragmatically asserted, should show it was cheaper for England to fight Hitler than the United States. "If England goes down to an honorable grave, there will be no one left to confront these Axis Powers except our own Government, and we shall have to spend $2.00 to $1.00 of theirs to build the same amount of armaments. If England falls, America will soon reach the time when our own efforts at preparation will destroy us." [15]

The problem of lend-lease to Great Britain, however, had become moot after Pearl Harbor. Once again Norris sat in the Senate and heard a President gravely request a declaration of war. This time the now-aged Nebraskan sadly voted for war. Norris always maintained that there was no inconsistency in his attitude toward the two war resolutions. The circumstances in 1917 and in 1941 were dissimilar; in 1917 there was no immediate threat of the war reaching American soil, whereas in 1941 an act of aggression had been committed against the United States.

Even before December 7, 1941, however, Norris had recognized that the character of the Führer's aggression was not the same as that of the Kaiser's machinations. In an article provocatively entitled "U.S. Must Save Britain Even if It Means War," he wrote:

We were, in my opinion, not justified in entering the last world war, but conditions which confronted us then have no similarity to the conditions which confront us now. At that time there was still honor among nations and men, even though they were enemies upon the battlefield. The enslavement of peoples was not then at stake. There was no likelihood that the life of our nation, as well as that of every other democracy in the world, would be endangered, no matter what the outcome of the war might be. There was no claim or belief in the mind of anyone that, if Germany won the war, it would be followed by a war in this hemi-

[15] *Ibid.* (February 13, 1941), Vol. 87, pt. 10, Appendix, p. 874.

sphere. However, in this war, we are confronted with an enemy whose ambitions are known to the world and that means destruction of every democracy in the world.[16]

Senator Norris' willingness to defend democracy even at the unhappy price of war was thoroughly consistent with his previous attitude, despite his first anti-war vote. As far back as 1916, when he opposed the Wilson preparedness program, he had conceded that war had often settled questions in the interest of liberty and humanity.[17] World War I had been instigated at the command of gold, and involved no humanitarian considerations, but World War II was a struggle to preserve democracy.

Although war might be justified, Norris still contended that recourse to war to solve international disputes was illogical, atavistic, and archaic. The greatest disgrace of the century was the fact that war between civilized nations remained a possibility. War, a relic of barbarism, was a condition painful "to every lover of humanity and to every believer in the great brotherhood of man." [18]

PEACE: THE IMAGE OF ETERNITY

George W. Norris, with his abiding faith in the wisdom of the common man, and his belief in the progress of civilization, entertained the hope that logic and humanity would ultimately triumph and war would become an unpleasant memory. Fully five years before the outbreak of World War I, and a decade in advance of the fight in the United States Senate over the confirmation of the Versailles settlements, Norris in a Chautauqua tour had advocated a League of Nations to prevent war and ensure permanent peace.[19] He did not, however, develop a systematic expression of his views until Europe was actually at war.

Arbitration to settle national disputes, he believed, was a manifestation of being civilized. Insofar as every civilized nation of the world required its subjects to submit their differences to law courts for settlement, there was no justifiable reason why kings and rulers

[16] *The Sunday Oregonian*, September 14, 1941.
[17] *Cong. Record*, 64th Cong., 1st sess. (July 13, 1916), Vol. 53, pt. 11, p. 10932.
[18] *Ibid.*, 65th Cong., 1st sess. (April 4, 1917), Vol. 55, pt. 1, p. 215.
[19] George W. Norris, *Fighting Liberal: The Autobiography of George W. Norris* (New York: The Macmillan Company, 1945), p. 203.

should settle their disputes on the battlefield. The ruling clique of the world should have begun to realize that sentiment for world peace had been growing rapidly for many years. "This is because the great common people of the world who have been compelled to fight the battle of kings and rulers have realized from their own experience and their own observation the unreasonableness and criminal folly of going to war." This sentiment for peace, Norris contended, had not come down from the throne but had come up from the people to the ruling classes. The time had come to build for international peace. Norris optimistically believed universal peace could be attained, for the passions of men were the same throughout the world. "Humanity is broader than nationality and embraces within its scope the entire world." [20] The English, French, Germans, and others, he said, would ultimately come to realize that there was no real enmity among them, only friendship.

However, Norris granted that the inherent friendship of people was subject to historical tensions that were the residue of barbarian times. The early national rulers had resorted to trickery, chicanery, and dishonesty in their attempts to conquer additional territory. This created mutual distrust among the nations which still permeated the framework of the whole European culture. But in the New World these conditions did not prevail. The divine right of kings and the right of conquest had been repudiated. America, thus, was unique among the nations of the world. "Our entire national life," Norris affirmed in the Senate, "has been emblematic of an unselfish respect for the right of other nations and is not tainted with that suspiciousness which has come down to others from ancient times." [21] As an example of this, Norris uncritically cited the role President Theodore Roosevelt had played in the termination of the Russo-Japanese War.[22]

In the midst of World War I, Norris contended that the world was ready for permanent peace. He suggested, accordingly, that, at the close of the struggle, the President of the United States, after having been duly authorized by Congress, should propose to

[20] *Cong. Record*, 64th Cong., 1st sess. (July 13, 1916), Vol. 53, pt. 11, p. 10931.
[21] *Ibid.* p. 10932.
[22] Norris, perhaps bedazzled by Theodore Roosevelt's subsequent Nobel Peace Prize, failed to recognize that TR's diplomacy during the Treaty of Portsmouth had been preceded by the secret Taft-Katsura memorandum and was a product of *Machtpolitik* rather than idealism.

the belligerent nations that the United States would be willing to enter into a treaty of peace with them. In such a treaty a permanent court of arbitration would be established for the settlement of all future international disputes. This treaty of peace would also provide for the limitation of both land and sea armament. An international navy would be maintained to enforce the decrees of the international court.

In elaborating the conditions for the establishment of a peace mechanism, Norris adopted as his model the Hague Permanent Court of Arbitration. In instances of national disagreement that could not be settled by diplomacy the contending parties would select a tribunal from a panel of this international court. Norris, at this time, believed that the judges of this court would be free from any bias and would dispense equal justice to any of the petitioning countries. Ultimately, the world would have a body of international jurists who would devote their full time and energies to the settlement of international disputes. Any question once determined by this great court would become a beacon light of peace for future generations.

It was indeed a sad commentary on modern civilization, he frequently argued, that the great nations of the world, while compelling their own citizens to submit their disputes to tribunals organized under general law, themselves violated the principles of the very law which they enforced upon their subjects. Norris with incredible naïveté believed that "the same principle of law and equity that settles an ordinary lawsuit before a justice of the peace will, if properly applied, without any change or addition, settle every dispute that can possibly arise between nations." [23]

Senator Norris, an idealist who accepted the American concept of mission, felt "the eternal hand of fate . . . beckoning for America to take the lead." "The American government," he boldly maintained, was "the one nation in all the world that can take the first step" in establishing permanent world harmony.[24] Yet when plans were proposed to help create an international league and establish arbitration courts, Norris vehemently opposed them. Essentially the Nebraskan based his opposition to the ratification of the peace treaty with Germany and the establishment of the League of Na-

[23] *Cong. Record*, 64th Cong., 1st sess. (July 13, 1916), Vol. 53, pt. 11, pp. 10932–33.
[24] *Ibid.*, 66th Cong., 1st sess. (July 15, 1919), Vol. 58, pt. 3, p. 2592.

tions on the contention that they were offensive to principles of justice. The Versailles Treaty, he moralized, was founded on no principle of equity, and contained within itself the seeds of wickedness and injustice. He insisted that the constitution for a League of Nations should concentrate only on those elements absolutely necessary to carry out the object of the compact. All other items would be extraneous and lend themselves to the creation of additional problems. Accordingly, the peacemakers should devote themselves to four major issues: the elimination of armament among nations, the abolition of conquest, the renunciation of secrecy in international relations, and the establishment of a mechanism of arbitration for disputes among nations.

In 1919, Senator Norris was not afraid that entering such a League of Nations would amount to a surrendering of America's sovereignty. Admittedly, complete liberty of action would be circumscribed by the constitution of the League; but this, he insisted, is something which is true of every agreement in civilization. "Absolute freedom in any civilized society can not be had, and the assertion and attempt to practice such freedom is anarchy. The only man who has complete personal liberty is the barbarian living alone in the woods." [25]

He was willing to include the Monroe Doctrine within the purview of the proposed League of Nations. In this respect, Norris was unlike many isolationists who feared that joining the League would mean that European nations henceforth might encroach upon exclusive American control of the Western Hemisphere. He argued that it would be acceptable to do this because the Monroe Doctrine would never have been promulgated had there been no secret treaties and secret agreements. The object of the Monroe Doctrine, he said, was to prohibit conquest within the Western Hemisphere by the nations of the Eastern Hemisphere. Norris, again contrary to prevalent isolationist sentiment, initially saw in the League a means whereby America might avoid entangling alliances.

Norris pointed out, however, that the Versailles Treaty contained not only a provision for a League of Nations, but also a remaking of the entire map of the world. It violated every sense of justice with the transfer of a great portion of the Chinese Em-

[25] *Ibid.*, p. 2593.

pire to Japan. Section 158 of the Treaty provided that all rights, privileges, and possessions of Germany in China would be turned over to Japan. The Senator strongly believed that the practical result of this provision would amount to giving Japan control over China. Germany initially had no right in China "that any honest man was bound to respect." This action transferred millions of innocent people to the rule and control of their worst enemy; it was violative of the principle of self-determination of peoples. Japan's bestial activities in Korea were a prelude to what would happen in China. The Nebraskan did not wish to build an international tribunal founded "upon the betrayal of any people, however weak." [26]

Not only was the transference of Chinese sovereignty to Japan wicked, but the procedure by which this was brought about was both reprehensible and indefensible, for it involved the use of secret diplomacy. The treaty then would be giving sanction to the employment of secret diplomacy. The secret treaties entered into by England, Japan, and France, by which Shantung was turned over to Japan, were in direct violation of the Fourteen Points, and particularly of that portion which provided for self-determination of peoples.

Norris wanted to strike article 10 from the treaty, because the real object of it was "to maintain the world supremacy of the British Empire, and the next object . . . to maintain the Japanese Empire." The Nebraskan, along with many others who had reservations about joining the League, was of the opinion that the British Empire would have too much voting power in the League. "It seems to me," Norris observed in the Senate, "that the wording of the document demonstrates beyond the possibility of doubt that this one Empire has in the League under this treaty six votes

[26] *Ibid.*, pp. 2593, 2595. On September 6, 1919, Senator Norris delivered in the Senate a lengthy and sometimes painfully obvious allegorical dissertation on the Shantung settlement which embodied a covert attack on President Wilson. The allegory had to do with characters whose identity was plain from the descriptive names given to them — Bill Kaiser, John Chinaman, Mr. Jap, Miss Korea, John Bull, Mr. French, Mr. Italiano, and Miss Columbia. These people lived in a place called the "Troubled Community." Bill Kaiser breaks loose and begins preying upon his neighbors. The allegory only incidentally touches upon the First World War; it is devoted to the Shantung seizure by Bill Kaiser and the subsequent course of Mr. Jap in driving out Bill Kaiser and his taking possession of Shantung for himself. *Cong. Record*, 66th Cong., 1st sess. (September 6, 1919), Vol. 58, pt. 5, pp. 4960–63.

as against any other nation whose representatives signed the treaty and which becomes a member of the League under the treaty." [27]

In a fervor of righteous indignation Norris emphasized that article 10 would not help the weak nations. It would only serve to uphold the cruel aristocratic reigns of greedy kings and pagan monarchs. Article 10 was inserted in order "to stifle the cry of freedom from Ireland . . . to keep in subjection the 400,000,000 of people in India . . . to compel Egypt to remain as a part of the British Empire . . . to nail down the coffin of Korea and hold Shantung in subjection to Japan." [28]

The Senator particularly opposed the treaty provisions concerning Egypt which he categorized as another Shantung. The same thing that Japan did when she took Korea had also been done by Great Britain in Egypt. But people were unaware of these things because censorship in London, Tokyo, and in Washington kept the world in ignorance of the crimes committed at Versailles in the name of peace.

Norris could not possibly sanction the treaty, because to do so would violate every principle for which the American forefathers fought. To condemn the treaty it was sufficient to know that every pledge made, by which hostilities were ended and the armistice signed, had been violated. One could not build a permanent peace upon a foundation of broken pledges. "This treaty, if approved," warned Norris, "while containing these inhuman and dishonorable things, will bring misery, suffering, and war to those who shall follow us, because they are in violation of nature's laws which are as immutable and unchangeable as the heavens." [29] The treaty as presented to the Senate, he dolefully predicted, "absolutely means future war." [30]

Although Norris rejected the Versailles Treaty he always looked for a royal road to peace. He unrealistically entertained a great

[27] Article 10 of the Covenant of the League of Nations provided: "The Members of the League undertake to respect and preserve as against external aggression the territorial integrity and existing political independence of all Members of the League. In case of any such aggression or in case of any threat or danger of such aggression the Council shall advise upon the means by which this obligation shall be fulfilled." *Ibid.* (November 11, 1919), Vol. 58, pt. 8, p. 8274. *Ibid.* (October 29, 1919), Vol. 58, pt. 8, p. 7688.
[28] *Ibid.* (November 11, 1919), Vol. 58, pt. 8, p. 8274.
[29] *Ibid.*, 66th Cong., 2d sess. (February 27, 1920), Vol. 59, pt. 4, p. 3576.
[30] *Ibid.*, 66th Cong., 1st sess. (October 13, 1919), Vol. 58, pt. 7, p. 6791.

deal of respect for the pet peace schemes of his distinguished fellow Nebraskan, William Jennings Bryan. The Senator maintained that the Bryan Peace Treaties were of great benefit to civilization and even ventured the opinion that "had such treaties existed between the nations of Europe there would have been no World War." The utility of the Bryan Peace Treaties, he thought, lay in the proposed waiting period during which time neither of the aggrieved countries would begin hostilities. During this waiting period "passion would be held back; reason and logic would be given an opportunity to operate." [31]

Although Senator Norris remained in favor of international cooperation as manifested in the Bryan Peace Treaties and disarmament conferences, the willingness with which he had previously endorsed an international tribunal began to wane in the 1920's. Norris' changed attitude toward a World Court was coincidental with his growing disillusionment and distrust of the European nations occasioned by the Versailles settlements and the disposition of the Allied war debts. In the mid-1920's the Nebraskan expressed a cautiously ambivalent attitude toward United States adherence to the World Court. In a statement to the *New York Times* he said:

Fundamentally I was in favor of the League of Nations, then came the Treaty of Versailles and the League of Nations Covenant. I had to vote against them because they did not do those things for which I could conscientiously give my vote. As to membership in the World Court, I do not believe the court is nearly as bad as its opponents paint it, nor as good as its friends say it is. Possibly it may do good, and I do not believe it can do us harm if we say we will not be bound to use force to enforce its decisions; if it does not entangle us in any way, and if we agree to take our cases before it when we, under our right, are willing to do so. [32]

[31] The Bryan treaties provided for the submission of all disputes to permanent commissions which would investigate the controversies for a period of one year. During this interval of investigation neither country would resort to war or increase its armament. After the completion of the investigation, the parties might accept or reject the commission's findings. Although war was not renounced, it was the intent of the treaties that peace would be maintained because of the "cooling-off" period. Bryan, as Secretary of State, negotiated thirty such agreements with Great Britain, France, Italy, and lesser powers in 1913 and 1914. George W. Norris, "Bryan as a Political Leader," *Current History*, XXII (September 1925), 860.
[32] *New York Times*, December 29, 1925, 2:6.

Some years later in a letter to Carrie Chapman Catt, honorary chairman of the National Committee on the Cause and Cure of War, Norris again conceded that the World Court was a good thing, but for Europe, not for the United States. One must never forget, he wrote, that the European nations were selfish and had pushed the United States into an unwanted foreign war. They had taken all the spoils of victory for themselves and were unwilling to return the money America had lent them to make their victory possible. The Nebraskan was convinced that Europe had only one use for America; that was to have the United States "at the sacrifice of human life and treasury make it possible for their selfish chestnuts to be pulled out of the international fire." Senator Norris' letter to Mrs. Catt continued, "I have seen this Court organized by nations, every one of which is jealous to a very high degree of our country. After we sacrificed the lives of many of our noblest citizens to help them out, they demanded that we cancel the debts which they owe us, and because we have been unwilling to do this, I am satisfied there had grown up among these selfish nations a hatred of the American Government which a fair investigation will demonstrate is bitter and relentless." [33]

Insofar as the World Court was a good thing for Europe, the Senator did not want to interfere with any movement or organization which would have a tendency to decide questions in dispute between nations in a court of reason rather than on the battlefield. He had voted for the World Court when the proposal was before the Senate for the first time, but he did so because of the reservations which had been attached. When the World Court proposal was again pending in the Senate in January 1935, Norris cautiously insisted on qualified membership, and introduced a reservation which called for "the express condition and understanding that no dispute or question in which the United States Government is a party shall be submitted to said Permanent Court of International Justice unless such submission has been approved by the United States Senate by a two-thirds vote." The Nebraskan was opposed to submitting all issues to the World Court, because "the nations of Europe are part of another form of civilization." He was reluctant to have the United States join an international court where "the

[33] Norris to Carrie Chapman Catt, March 7, 1932, Norris Papers. These sentiments were part of a form letter used by the Senator's office at that time.

judges are men who have lived under different conditions, who have different ideas of society, who have different ideas of government, who come in the main from different kinds of governments than under which we live." [34] Norris feared that these cultural differences would create a bias against the United States in the determination of some questions to which the United States was a party. The Roosevelt administration reacted promptly to the Norris reservation. At his press conference the President denounced it as a definite limitation on the constitutional powers of the President. And in the Senate, Senator Robinson argued against it. The Administration logic prevailed and the Norris reservation was defeated the same day it was submitted.

Senator Norris' post–World War I distrust of unqualified adherence to a permanent world court represents a departure from his previous attitude toward international arbitration. In 1916 when Norris first systematically developed his ideas concerning a world court, he had not been worried about American loss of sovereignty, or about national interests influencing the tribunal. He believed that the court would be removed from the currents of international power politics. But the experience of World War I and the peace settlement soured him. He now recognized that international politics were immoral. "During the war," he explained in a letter to a constituent, he had had his "eyes opened to many things which . . . demonstrated that our Allies were not always acting in good faith." A clear indication of Allied bad faith, Norris thought, was the war debt problem. This only proved that the European nations were not to be trusted and that the United States should not enter the World Court without reservations. He agreed with President Coolidge's myopic view that the Europeans had "hired the money." They were legally and morally obligated to repay it. To Norris the entire debt question was summed up in the proposition "whether the American taxpayer or the European taxpayer shall pay these debts." The Senator was opposed to all the settlements made with European nations because America had made those loans under a statute which clearly defined the conditions. The American government had borrowed the money from its citizens, now the European nations were failing to live up to their obligations. It

[34] *Cong. Record*, 74th Cong., 1st sess. (January 25, 1935), Vol. 79, pt. 1, p. 965.

would be better to forgive some of the debts entirely than to accept the settlements that were made. Italy, Norris charged, boasted that she headed the world in military air strength. If it were not for Italy's military preparations she then would be able to repay the United States. France was also guilty; she refused to pay America even interest, but she had carried on an African war and had supplied men, money, and munitions to Poland. The Young Plan and the Dawes Plan, furthermore, were makeshifts "brought about mostly by the international bankers." [35]

Neither the pressure of domestic troubles, nor foreign aggression against the European democracies induced Norris to change his attitude regarding the debt question. In an attempt to ameliorate the widespread agricultural depression of the early 1930's, Henry A. Wallace, future New Deal Secretary of Agriculture, and then editor of his family's influential agricultural periodical *Wallace's Farmer*, wrote to Senator Norris suggesting that it might be wise to go along with President Hoover's war debt moratorium, because "it fits in with the fight we in the midwest are making for an honest dollar and higher prices." The Nebraskan was unimpressed with Wallace's logic and in his reply reiterated his position that the European nations were not acting in good faith. America was "paying through taxation for the building of armaments, battleships, etc. . . . by these foreign nations." [36] In the spring of 1940, when Hitler's *Blitzkreig* ended the "phony war," Democratic Representative Andrew J. May of Kentucky, chairman of the House Military Affairs Committee, urged the relaxation of the Johnson Act which banned American credits or loans to nations which had defaulted on their World War I debts. Norris strenuously attacked May's proposal and stressed his economic-interest theme that the best way to become embroiled in a foreign war would be to permit America to become financially involved overseas. [37]

Although Norris was greatly disillusioned by the Versailles Treaty, and exceedingly critical of the European powers for defaulting on their war debts, he nonetheless continued to recognize

[35] Norris to: John W. Little, January 20, 1926; L. T. Youngsblood, May 15, 1926; H. N. Jewett, May 22, 1925; C. G. Binderup, December 29, 1931, Norris Papers.
[36] Henry A. Wallace to Norris, December 18, 1931; Norris to Wallace, January 21, 1932, Norris Papers.
[37] *New York Times*, May 13, 1940, 1:2.

the necessity for international cooperation. A year after the aged Marshal Pétain had surrendered France to the Germans and a week before Hitler launched his attack against the Soviet Union, Senator Norris, in a commencement address delivered at Wooster College, Ohio, in June 1941, warned against repeating the mistakes of Versailles, and optimistically philosophized about the peace which would come after the overthrow of the Axis powers. "The peace which should follow the destruction of Hitler and his pagan philosophy of government," he opined, "should be one which will give prominence to the liberality of the conqueror in the day of his victory." America should sit down with the victors at the peace table and help construct a world order founded on human love and brotherhood. It should be a peace which would include no reparations or indemnities which would mean the sentencing "of the conquered people to a life of servitude." The peace should call for complete disarmament of Germany and the restoration of all the conquered nations. England and the restored nations should be called in conference to make an effort to bring about universal disarmament. Norris, now an octogenarian, still believed that "if the world is disarmed everlasting peace will follow." [88]

During World War II the Senator reaffirmed his belief that the successful termination of the conflict would bring a new opportunity to create a peace that would be carved "in the image of eternity." In a lecture at the University of Nebraska he presented a broad outline of the principles underlying the future settlement to be concluded at the cessation of the then current hostilities. A permanent peace must be established, he reasoned, because "this impoverished, battered world of ours cannot afford the luxury and the crime of a third world war." Despite the nature of the war, the

[88] George W. Norris, "A Pagan Philosophy of Government," Commencement Address at Wooster College, Ohio, June 10, 1941, reprinted in *Cong. Record*, 77th Cong., 1st sess. (June 16, 1941), Vol. 87, pt. 12, Appendix, p. 2862. In an interview with a *New York Times* reporter on the occasion of his eightieth birthday, Norris gave a homely and exceedingly unsophisticated illustration of the evil effects of armament. He told his interviewer that once he had a cow who possessed a very fine pair of horns; but because of those horns she was a mean animal. Norris related that he "went to a neighbor who had a dehorning machine and asked him to come down and dehorn that cow . . . she lost her armament . . . she didn't want to fight anymore. It's the same way with nations. When they are disarmed and get used to it, they are only too glad to go back to their peaceful way of living." Harold Hinton, "This Is Not Like 1917 — Says Norris," *New York Times Magazine*, July 6, 1941, p. 7.

Allies must guard against violence producing violence, and hate breeding hate. "Restraint of the determination for revenge," he counseled, "is one of the sacrifices we must impose upon ourselves." It was only by contemplating the future and thinking in terms of endless time that the Allies would find "the strength, the inspiration, and the vision to restrain the natural impulses . . . and forego revenge upon enemies who do not deserve mercy." [39]

The prime requisite for a lasting peace, he emphasized, would be the imposition of complete disarmament upon the subjugated enemy. "The predominating and the great preliminary step in the attainment of perpetual peace," Norris always insisted, "was the outlawing of those weapons which make war possible." [40] Manufacture of all kinds of military weapons must be made impossible by the complete destruction of every plant devoted to war production. The victorious Allies must instill into the hearts of the vanquished Axis the recognition that their disarmament is necessary for the peace of the world. Initially the Allies would have to police the aggressor countries, but this would be only for a period of fifty or sixty years. An international commission could be established with adequate power and facilities to investigate any possible move to violate the disarmament provisions of the treaty. Ultimately, the Nebraskan was certain, the problem of disarmament would take care of itself. One must have faith in America and her allies if perpetual peace was to be achieved.

In addition to disarmament, Norris maintained, the victor nations must not demand of the defeated aggressor nations unconscionable indemnities. The defeated nations must be given time to recover and to rehabilitate their peacetime productive capacities. All war debts should be repudiated for two reasons. First, repudiation would have a tendency to cause the financier, who furnished the money for war and profited by war, to hesitate before he loaned money to any nation that set out to conquer the world.

[39] George W. Norris, *Peace Without Hate* (Lincoln: University of Nebraska Press, 1943), pp. 36, 12, 18, 23. The spirit of charity, however, did not preclude the punishment of war criminals. Where there had been a wanton violation of ordinary conceptions of justice and decency, the course was clear and simple. "Those men," wrote Norris in his Autobiography, "who are guilty should be brought to trial. Punishment should be meted out based upon the conceptions of justice which have governed civilization in its wisdom." Norris, *Fighting Liberal, op. cit.*, p. 384.
[40] Norris, *Peace, op. cit.*, p. 20.

Second, it would permit the aggressor nations to pay a larger sum into the indemnity chest to help reimburse the Allied nations for some of the losses which they had sustained.

But the supreme obligation of the Allies was to be Good Samaritans, to feed the starving and clothe the naked. America must take the lead in hope of restoring a tortured world to plenty and to peace. The burden of peace which America and the Allies must want is the burden of helping the enemy to his feet. The concept of *lex talionis* — an eye for an eye and a tooth for a tooth — must be forgotten. America must lead the Allies in building a peace without hate.

A peace without hate, Norris believed, could be established through international cooperation. In one of his last published articles he advocated the postwar creation of some sort of League of Nations which would be open to all the countries of the world, including Germany.[41] But the Senator never lived to see the Allied victory and the establishment of the United Nations. Whether or not he would have agreed with the details of the peace settlement following World War II would be dangerous speculation at best. One, nevertheless, can be certain that he would have agreed to many of the principles embodied in the Charter of the United Nations.

This vision which George W. Norris displayed in domestic matters, for the most part, was not carried over into foreign affairs. He had little understanding of the varied and complex forces in world history. Although he had spent many years in Washington, many of his attitudes on international questions were provincial. He was unable to understand the political shadings involved in foreign relations and saw policies as either good or bad. His devil theory explanation of America's entrance into the First World War, an explanation from which he never retreated, was as incorrect as it was elemental. One cannot reduce the multiple causes of international conflict to the nefarious activities of Wall Street and the arms and munitions makers. His intransigence on the war debt issue can be explained, but it cannot be excused. And during the torpid inter-war years his vigorous opposition to the League of Nations and unqualified adherence to the World Court — a retreat from

[41] George W. Norris, "Germany After Defeat," *New Republic*, CX (May 22, 1944), 704.

his former forward and positive internationalist stance — while perhaps misplaced, nonetheless were based on the highest of motives, Senator Norris' obdurate opposition to the Wilsonian proposals never stemmed from a desire for partisan political advantage or from personal animosity. It is well to remember that many of the liberals, who like Norris actively supported domestic reform, also deserted the Wilson camp. Thus for example, Oswald Garrison Villard of *The Nation* and Herbert Croly of the *New Republic*, the two editors who personified and articulated liberal thought, refused to accept the Wilson panaceas.[42]

Yet although Senator Norris rejected American participation in the League of Nations he always affirmed his faith in human rights and international brotherhood, and always opposed the scourge of war. He carried into his conception of world politics a confidence in the democratic processes of logic, reason, and law, and a humanistic belief in the brotherhood of man. His philosophy of world democracy was conditioned by his rigorous concept of moral justice and tended to be a combination of idealism and naïveté. His peace panaceas lacked sophistication because he unquestioningly assumed that the nations of the world would readily accept disarmament. Senator Norris, unfortunately, lacked a mature understanding of the intricacies of foreign affairs and the complex subtleties of international power politics.

Nonetheless, one should not castigate him too harshly. His greatest energies were directed toward solving pressing national problems. And certainly his sincerity remains unquestioned. If, like Isaiah, he longed for a civilization in which nation no longer warred against nation and there were no swords and no spears but only plowshares and pruning-hooks, he held a vision worth dreaming.

[42] For an excellent exposition of the liberal defection from Wilsonian idealism, see Selig Adler, *The Isolationist Impulse: Its Twentieth-Century Reaction* (London and New York: Abelard-Schuman Ltd., 1957), pp. 54–75.

CHAPTER SIX

A Democrat Appraised

GEORGE W. NORRIS AND THE PROGRESSIVE SPIRIT

The general proposition that as one grows older he generally departs from the more liberal political attitudes of his youth and becomes more conservative in his thinking never applied to George W. Norris. The opposite, in fact, occurred with him. Not only did he begin his political career as a Republican, but he began it in an area and at a time in which the angry tide of Populism was beginning to reach its apogee. He lost the contest for his first political office, county district attorney, primarily because as a Republican he could not successfully compete against Populist sentiment. In his other campaigns for state office, however, although running as a Republican, he received some Populist support. And when he ran for Congress for the first time in 1902 he based his campaign on the contention that he was a farmer and "The Poor Man's Friend." Thus, Norris arrived in Washington as a Republican, but he carried with him tinges of Populism. These Populist leanings, which came to him in middle age, remained latent during his first few years as a congressman, and were elaborated and modified in his later life so as to blend into the prevailing twentieth-century American political reform tradition. When Norris first arrived in

Washington as a representative in 1903, the climate was astir with
the disclosures of muckraking, then just beginning to be militant.
In time the major premises of muckraking — honesty in government, the democratization of the political process, the restriction
of big business, and the conservation of natural resources — began
to take hold of the Nebraskan. By the Bankers' Panic of 1907,
Norris, with his strong midwestern agricultural sentiments, had
developed a pronounced distaste for the conservative Eastern wing
of the Republican party. In 1909 he was instrumental in defeating
Speaker Joseph G. Cannon in his attempt to control the House
Committee which was to investigate the Ballinger-Pinchot controversy. And a year later he spearheaded the Insurgent-Democratic
coalition which destroyed the Speaker's arbitrary power to appoint
members of the strategic Rules Committee. Toward the end of
his years as a representative, the initially conservative Norris had
become identified with the rising spirit of progressivism.

The 1912 campaign in which Norris ran for his first Senate seat
was a political and intellectual watershed. In it the progressive
movement reached its fullest and finest expression, yet simultaneously diverged into the philosophies and programs set forth by
Theodore Roosevelt's New Nationalism and Woodrow Wilson's
New Freedom. But Norris' intellectual commitment to the New
Nationalism, although he had supported Roosevelt, was no greater
than his commitment to the New Freedom. This was so because he
subscribed to an ideology which was essentially contoured by
Populist doctrines. Norris was able to accept some of the rationale
of both Roosevelt and Wilson because a great deal of progressive
political effort was spent enacting proposals that the Populists had
outlined earlier. The only position with which the Senator found
no sympathy during the tumultuous 1912 campaign was that of
Eugene V. Debs. Norris could not then, and never did, agree with
the fundamental socialist premise that "the capitalist system has
outgrown its historical function, and has become utterly incapable
of meeting the problems . . . confronting society."[1]

Norris reasoned that the ordinary honest hard-working farmer

[1] The only plank in the Bull Moose Platform which was not in accord with
Norris' thinking was the demand for the short ballot. Norris rejected any
attrition of the people's sovereignty. In contrast, both Roosevelt and Wilson
believed that, although the short ballot compressed the range of elective
offices presented to the voters, in actual effect, the government would be
more responsible to the people because the lines of accountability would be

and laborer were entitled to a fair return for their toil. The Nebraskan agreed with the Populist contention that there must be "wrong
and crime and fraud somewhere" when the people were denied
the results of their own labors. He accepted the premise, consequently, that the blame for this unjust situation rested with the
giant trusts, the railroads, the manufacturers, the middlemen, and
the Wall Street financiers. The government must bring about a
redress of grievances in order to destroy these oppressors of the
people, but the agencies of government were controlled by the plutocrats and their lackeys, the political bosses. To achieve corrective
legislation, therefore, the government must be returned to the
people through the use of mechanical and institutional reform.
Norris unequivocally accepted what Hicks has called the two fundamental Populist principles: "One, that the government must
restrain the selfish tendencies of those who profited at the expense
of the poor and the needy; the other, that the people, not the plutocrats, must control the government."

With respect to both of these broad assumptions Theodore
Roosevelt's Progressive platform of 1912 and Woodrow Wilson's
Democratic platform of the same year were in general agreement.
The Bull Moose "Covenant with the People" proclaimed the need
"for equal opportunity and industrial justice" and pledged itself to
destroy the invisible government of the plutocracy so as "to dissolve the unholy alliance between corrupt business and corrupt
politics." And the Democratic platform, with equal righteousness,
not only avowed that "private monopoly is indefensible and intol-
erable," but also called for vigorous enforcement of civil and
criminal law against trusts and unequivocally demanded "the

clearer. The section of the Progressive Platform dealing with business was
written in very general terms and called for a strengthening of the Sherman
Act. Norris was able to endorse the trust plank because of its broadness. Progressive Platform of 1912, in Kirk H. Porter and Donald Bruce Johnson, compilers, *National Party Platforms: 1840–1960* (Urbana: University of Illinois
Press, 1961), p. 175. Socialist Platform of 1912, in *ibid.*, p. 188. Norris, once
queried as to his beliefs on socialism, replied, "From what little study I have
made of socialism, I have reached the conclusion that I would not favor such
a step unless I was drawn to it by the failure of any other way to meet some
of the great problems which confront us as a people. At the present time I
would confine government ownership and operation to some of the public
utility activities, for instance, the public ownership and control of the water
in municipalities and the generation, transmission, and distribution of electricity, and perhaps others." Norris to Paul S. Jacobson, March 7, 1936, Norris Papers.

enactment of such additional legislation as to make it impossible for a private monopoly to exist in the United States." [2]

Despite their similarity — both the New Nationalism and the New Freedom were devoted to the cause of social justice — their methods and philosophies differed. The underlying premises of TR's New Nationalism were conditioned by, if not derived from, Herbert Croly's *The Promise of American Life*, and stressed urban, Eastern, Hamiltonian sources. The New Nationalism, instead of eradicating the trust, would allow it to exist, but it would be controlled for democratic ends. Inequality and bigness were natural consequences of industrialism. The federal government, accordingly, was to subject the large corporations to public control; laissez-faire was to be abandoned for governmental protection. Woodrow Wilson, in contrast, still imbued with nineteenth-century laissez-faire concepts, believed that the preservation of economic freedom must be achieved by different means. Independent business must be set free from the restrictions of monopoly and special privilege. The New Freedom, for Wilson, was to be a rebirth of the old freedom; it was to use the instrument of the state to destroy the artificial barriers imposed by monopolies against the full development of the individual's energies. Government, reasoned the professor in the White House, should restore individual competition; it should provide freedom from the trust for the small business, as well as protection for the farmer against the banker, the manufacturer, and the transportation monopoly, and for the employee against the employer.[3]

The philosophy of economic freedom which President Wilson

[2] John D. Hicks, *The Populist Revolt: A History of the Farmers' Alliance and the People's Party* (Minneapolis: University of Minnesota Press, 1931), pp. 403, 406. Porter and Johnson, *op. cit.*, p. 169. William Allen White, in overstating the case for progressivism as a direct lineal descendant of Populism, picturesquely observed that the progressives "caught the Populists in swimming and stole all their clothing except the frayed underdrawers of free silver." George E. Mowry, *The Progressive Movement, 1900–1920: Recent Ideas and New Literature* (Washington D.C.: American Historical Association, 1958), p. 3.

[3] Professor Mowry discounts the influence of Croly on Roosevelt. ". . . Roosevelt may have had as much influence on Croly as Croly had on him." George E. Mowry, *The Era of Theodore Roosevelt: 1900–1912* (New York: Harper and Brothers, 1958), p. 222. See also: Harris I. Effross, *The Political Philosophy of Herbert Croly* (unpublished Ph.D. thesis, Rutgers University, 1959). Arthur S. Link, *Woodrow Wilson and the Progressive Era: 1910–1917* (New York: Harper and Brothers, 1954), pp. 1–81.

articulated had been conditioned by his association with Louis D. Brandeis, the leading progressive lawyer and future Supreme Court justice, who became one of Wilson's closest advisers in the 1912 campaign. Brandeis, prior to the hectic Progressive nominations, had supported La Follette and had campaigned strenuously in the Republican primary for Norris. Brandeis had emphasized for Norris the fact that the trusts and industrial despotism made economic democracy impossible, and without economic democracy political democracy could not endure. In many ways Brandeis and Norris thought alike. Each wanted to abolish corporate giantism which created monopoly and fostered irresponsibility. They agreed that labor unions should be protected in their right to use collective bargaining, and that men, women, and children should not be forced to labor excessively. Brandeis, however, went much further than Norris in working out these ideas. Norris proposed that the government create work, if necessary, in order to keep labor employed, but he never went as far as Brandeis' demand that labor be entitled as a matter of equity to participate in company decisions and to receive a guaranteed annual wage. They also disagreed on public ownership; Brandeis was opposed to all forms of government ownership, while Norris was willing to permit the government to enter the economy in certain areas.

Although Wilson subscribed to many of the teachings of Brandeis, the urban, sophisticated, well-trained intellectual, he also cultivated William Jennings Bryan and, in recognition of political exigencies, appointed him Secretary of State. Bryan was the antithesis of the quiet scholarly Brandeis and the fiercely moralistic Wilson, but the Great Commoner, as his sobriquet indicates, was unique among the leaders of the progressive movement in that he embodied the popular feelings which the other progressive leaders sensed and fashioned.[4]

While Bryan, Roosevelt, Wilson, La Follette, and Norris were all progressives, in the sense that they articulated a common desire to help the average American and were willing to use the forces of government to achieve this goal, they nevertheless differed in their attitudes and techniques. Roosevelt had leisure-class tastes

[4] Edward McNall Burns, *The American Idea of Mission: Concepts of National Purpose and Destiny* (New Brunswick: Rutgers University Press, 1957), pp. 182–84. Richard Hofstadter, *The American Political Tradition* (New York: Vintage Books, 1954), p. 187.

and a patrician sense of *noblesse oblige*. Wilson was austere and didactic. Norris came closest to a combination of Bryan and La Follette, also midwesterners.

Though Norris, like his fellow Nebraskan Bryan, often lacked sophistication and expressed popular ideology, he rose above the intellectual level of the Great Commoner. Norris refined the concepts which Bryan preached and augmented them to meet some of the newly created demands of a rapidly urbanizing, industrializing society. While Norris perceived the shadows of social change, Bryan was never able to surmount his agrarian intellectual preconceptions. Bryan early became famous for his advocacy of monetary heresy — the inimitable Cross of Gold speech at the Democratic Convention of 1896 — and later for his advocacy of religious orthodoxy — the Scopes "monkey" trial — but Norris never unduly concerned himself with either the coinage of silver or the practice of religion. Norris and Bryan also differed in that the former was actively concerned with the problems of labor while the latter never sponsored a positive program of labor legislation or had, as Hofstadter notes, "any clear conception of the trials of working-class existence." [5] The two Nebraskans differed further on the crucial role of political parties. The Peerless Leader did not insist, as did Norris, that parties thwarted democracy. But Norris and Bryan were one in their insistence that agriculture was fundamental and that the people of the United States had sufficient intelligence to pass judgment on all political issues because these issues were essentially of a moral nature, and both men shared a deep and optimistic sense of America's mission. Norris, however, came closest to Robert Marion La Follette of Wisconsin who, for many liberals, epitomized the mainstream of the progressive movement before and after World War I. The life of La Follette, six years the senior of Norris, in many ways paralleled that of the Nebraskan. Both, while still small children, sustained the death of a father. Both knew the discomforts and miseries of poverty. Both struggled through college under a financial burden. Though the pattern of their early political careers diverged, they later merged. Norris worked with the Republican machine until his insurgency and the Cannon fight, and even after that, never repudiated the Republican label until his Independent candidacy in 1936.

[5] *Ibid.*, p. 190.

The Wisconsin Progressive, on the other hand, entered politics by bucking the local machine and throughout his political life battled the organizations of both major parties. They disagreed drastically, moreover, on the important matter of the efficacy of a third party. La Follette believed that third parties, organized in the interests of the people, were necessary vehicles through which the common man could secure control of the government. Norris, however, had small faith in any party. He always pessimistically reasoned that in time the new parties would become as bad as the old parties unless the leaders of these new third parties "were Christ-like men in which case they would not be political leaders." [6]

La Follette accepted the premise that the voice of the people should be the will of the government; but, somewhat antimoniously to this populistic idea of democracy, he also propounded the Wisconsin Idea, which stressed the role of the university-trained government expert. Democracy and reform, La Follette believed, could only be achieved when the voters had complete control of the elective machinery. Numerous measures, accordingly, were necessary to remove the restrictions on the power of the people. He accepted the direct government devices of the initiative, referendum, recall, direct primary, the abolition of the electoral college, and the direct election of the President and Vice-President. He also proposed extending some of these devices to the judiciary, in order to restrict severely the power of judicial review and to have elective federal judgeships. Norris strongly agreed with these direct government measures and in his years in the Senate tried various ways of bringing them about.

Both Norris and La Follette, along with Bryan, were nurtured in the intellectual traditions of the Midwest which were rooted, in part, in Jeffersonian and Jacksonian sources. They believed in the solid virtues of frontier equality, individualism, and the common man. But at the same time they departed radically from Jeffersonian ideals, particularly the conception of limited government. They favored, instead, positive government, because they feared concentration and control, and its concomitant, unregulated industrial bigness.

[6] The solution to this political dilemma was not the creation of new parties but rather the elimination of the cumbrous machinery of the electoral college. See *supra*, Chapter Two. George W. Norris, "Put Not Your Faith in Parties," *The Nation*, CXVIII (April 3, 1924), 369.

While Theodore Roosevelt and Woodrow Wilson became famous, respectively, for their New Nationalism and New Freedom, both programs of an urban, Eastern character, George Norris and Robert La Follette followed an agrarian midwestern philosophy which the Wisconsin progressive, Charles McCarthy, called the New Individualism. The New Individualism attempted to evolve a democratic capitalistic society free from both the evils of ruthless individualism and the regimentation of socialism and communism. It was a middle path between the two extremes. This middle path, paradoxically, received its most forceful articulation during the 1920's when Harding-Coolidge mediocrity and conservatism seemed to pervade the country. Although the reform spirit languished and was eclipsed after World War I, it was not dead. It was revived by the People's Legislative Service, the Progressive Conference of 1922, and the Conference for Progressive Political Action which launched the Progressive party in the 1924 campaign.[7]

In that year, although opposed to the creation of a third party, Senator Norris nonetheless endorsed his friend "Battling Bob" La Follette when he was nominated for the Presidency by the Progressives at their evangelical convention in Cleveland. Support for the Robert M. La Follette–Burton K. Wheeler ticket came from diverse sources. Veterans of old protest causes, General Jacob Coxey, editor John Streeter, who, writes William E. Leuchtenburg, "wore a flowing beard because he had taken an oath in the 1890's not to shave until Populism was victorious," and others joined forces with spokesmen of the newer urban progressivism such as Fiorello LaGuardia, who told the convention that he had come "to let you know that there are other streets and other attitudes in New York besides Wall Street. I speak for Avenue A and 116th Street, instead of Broad and Wall." The midwestern candidates

[7] Charles McCarthy (1873–1921) organized and directed the Wisconsin Legislative Reference Library, the intellectual fountain of much of the progressive legislation enacted in Wisconsin during the gubernatorial administration of Robert La Follette. See Charles McCarthy, *The Wisconsin Idea* (New York: The Macmillan Company, 1912). This definition of New Individualism is a paraphrase of Professor Nye's definition. For an excellent discussion not only of the New Individualism, but also of the intellectual currents preceding Populism and progressivism, particularly in relation to their impact on midwestern thinking, see Russel B. Nye, *Midwestern Progressive Politics: A Historical Study of Its Origins and Development, 1870–1958* (East Lansing: Michigan State University Press, 1959).

also received the blessings of the Executive Council of the American Federation of Labor and the Socialist party.[8]

The La Follette–Wheeler platform of 1924 was reminiscent of the 1912 Bull Moose Armageddon in that it too proposed a "Covenant with the People" and postulated the great issue before the American people as "the control of government and industry by private monopoly." Its major planks called for: public ownership of the nation's railroads and water power; "the creation and development of a national superpower system, including Muscle Shoals, to supply at actual cost light and power for the people and nitrate for the farmers"; a taxation policy which would reduce taxes on moderate incomes and increase inheritance taxes; the direct election of all federal judges for fixed terms of not longer than ten years; legislation for the relief of agriculture; the abolition of the injunction in labor disputes; ratification of the Child Labor Amendment; the creation of a St. Lawrence Seaway; sundry popular sovereignty measures such as direct nomination and election of the President, extending the initiative and referendum to the federal government, insuring "a popular referendum for or against war except in cases of actual invasion"; and a foreign policy which would revise the Versailles Treaty, promote agreements to outlaw wars, abolish conscription, drastically reduce armaments, and "guarantee public referendum on peace and war." [9]

This Progressive program, in its most sweeping outlines, was the New Individualism. In some aspects it was gravely deficient:

[8] William E. Leuchtenburg, *The Perils of Prosperity: 1914–1932* (Chicago: University of Chicago Press, 1958), p. 132. For an analysis of progressivism in 1924, see Kenneth Campbell MacKay, *The Progressive Movement of 1924* (New York: Columbia University Press, 1947). For LaGuardia's attitudes, see Arthur Mann, *LaGuardia: A Fighter Against His Times, 1882–1933* (Philadelphia: J. B. Lippincott Co., 1959), p. 171.

[9] La Follette's Platform of 1924, in Porter and Johnson, *op. cit.*, p. 253. The Conference for Progressive Political Action also issued a platform which was practically identical with La Follette's program. See Conference for Progressive Political Action Platform, 1924, in *ibid.*, pp. 255–56. In 1924 Norris agreed with La Follette on the merits of a popular referendum for or against war. In answer to a questionnaire sent out by the Nebraska Conference for Progressive Political Action Norris responded, "I believe that we ought to provide for a referendum before we go to war." However, in 1940 when "Young Bob" La Follette, following his illustrious father's footsteps, proposed in the Senate that a federal referendum be held on the war question, Norris voted against this proposal. Norris to Nebraska Conference for Progressive Political Action, August 12, 1924, Norris Papers.

in its uncritical acceptance and apotheosation of folkish democracy; in its strident insistence and simplification of a primitive conspiracy theory of economics and politics at home; and in its incredibly unsophisticated appreciation, understanding, and explanation of international relations. Nonetheless, it was extremely significant and viable in its treatment of conservation, taxation, agriculture, labor, and the St. Lawrence Seaway; not only did it represent a throwback — both good and bad — to preceding dissident movements, but it also embodied a sensitive and dynamic program for the present and a visionary plan for the future. The attack by Norris and the other progressives was not against the essentials of capitalism, but rather its operation, and its failure to measure up to their standards. They wanted to keep capitalism, while controlling its abuses. The Norris–La Follette progressives wanted to eliminate the tariffs and railroad rates which oppressed the farmer, and the injunctions, court decisions, and tax policy which harassed the laborer. Accordingly, certain collectivistic measures were advocated. While the New Individualism accepted public ownership and management in the area of natural monopolies and in fields where monopolies might exist to public detriment, it also advocated regulation by commission and rigid taxing policies. Norris never thought in terms of fundamental Marxist dogma such as a socialization of all the means of production; and he certainly opposed collectivization of land, a dictatorship of the proletariat, and the achievement of a classless society.

In short, the drift of midwestern progressive thought as embodied in the Norris–La Follette New Individualism was a departure from the traditional Jeffersonian-Jacksonian concepts. The ends remained much the same but the methods changed as the frontier faded. Norris, and others like him, had to reconcile the old eighteenth-century ideal of untrammeled individualism with nineteenth- and twentieth-century problems of an industrial urban society. In doing so the New Individualists grafted onto the intellectual shibboleths of Jefferson and Jackson the concept of a positive state responsive to the needs of a broad-based electorate. Norris was forced to shift from pure individualism toward government control, but this did not imply socialism; collectivistic restriction on laissez-faire, as proposed by Norris, was a device to preserve capitalism itself.

The power of the state was to be used both negatively and positively. The negative use of government machinery implied antitrust laws to control corporate concentration, the supervision of transportation facilities, a tax policy which emphasized high inheritance and corporation taxes, banking and insurance laws, public service and utility commissions, and other regulatory measures. The positive use of government machinery implied the enactment of social-justice legislation such as workmen's compensation and employers' liability laws, industrial safety standards, wage and hour laws, old-age pensions, and other legislation designed to ameliorate onerous working conditions. Government was to act as the conscience of insensate industrialism.

In short, Norris retained much of the Bryan thinking of 1896 — faith in the common man and the belief that political questions essentially were moral questions, an agrarian fundamentalism, a lingering suspicion of the cities, and a vehement hatred of monopoly, Wall Street, and big business. To these attitudes he added some of the thinking of Roosevelt and Wilson in 1912 — a realization of the problems of the city and an awareness of the needs which inspired the social-justice movement. But Norris' acceptance of the New Individualism, moreover, went beyond tacitly recognizing the workingman's right in society. The labor legislation for which he became famous — the Norris-LaGuardia Act — also bears the name of Fiorello LaGuardia, a symbol of the urban immigrant. Norris was seemingly the antithesis of LaGuardia in his belief that agriculture was the cornerstone of society, but they both shared a sincere desire to improve the lot of the common man. The Senator, despite his agrarian bias, nonetheless recognized the importance of the laborer. This recognition of the complementary nature of the farm and the city enabled Norris to work with both the urban and rural segments of the progressive movement before and after World War I.

But in the twenties, the New Individualism's appeal, heeded with a religious fervor by the devoted few, had only a limited impact on the multitude of the electorate. The statistics of the 1924 election are revealing: Coolidge swept the country with 15 million votes; Davis was a poor second with 8 million votes; and La Follette, with less than 5 million votes, trailed. In twelve years an incredible change had taken place in America. The spirit of reform which had prevailed in 1912 had been replaced in 1924, for the most part, with unfeeling complacency engendered by a material-istic ethic and a general escalation of economic prosperity. Pro-gressivism foundered. The movement, encompassing a host of viewpoints and racked with tensions, had difficulty focusing upon a common program. When La Follette died, exhausted and bit-ter, shortly after the election, Norris was presented with a signal opportunity to rally, mobilize, and reorganize the progressive forces. But the Nebraskan did not do this. His unswerving personal antipathy to any political organization — even one led by himself, which he would have recognized to be in the interests of all the people — was too strong.

In retrospect one can carp at Norris for failing to recognize that the way to viable political power is through the medium of political parties. Much as Hoover was inhibited in combatting the Depression by his deep-seated convictions and neutral (as opposed to vigorous) view of the Presidency, so too, Norris was inhibited, by another set of predilections, from implementing his liberal views. George Norris' failure to properly appreciate and understand the role and value of a democratically organized and oriented political party, along with his oversimplification and uncritical emphasis on a conspiracy interpretation of domestic and foreign affairs, were his greatest intellectual liabilities.

Nonetheless, as a forceful and dynamic leader of the Senate "Sons of the Wild Jackass," Norris kept the progressive spirit alive and in the national conscience in matters relating to agriculture and hydroelectric development and expansion. The agricultural subsidization plans associated with McNary-Haugenism, despite their temporary lack of acceptance, represented "a milestone in the development of a comprehensive political doctrine that it was government's duty to protect the economic security of all classes and particularly depressed ones." And Norris' long and bitter fight for the orderly development of the Tennessee Valley epitomized the progressive struggle for public control of the burgeoning power industry. "The maturing of an advanced farm program and the formulation of plans for public power and regional develop-ments," Arthur S. Link has perceptively noted, "may be termed the two most significant progressive achievements on the national level in the 1920's." [10]

In both these areas, as well as labor reform legislation, the Senator was an acknowledged leader. And of these, regional development in the Tennessee Valley and workingmen's legislation had but a minimal effect on his constituency. The philosophy underlying these progressive battles of the 1920's was vindicated, accepted, and put into practice in the troubled 1930's by the New Deal. And much of the credit for this triumph belongs to Norris.

A DREAMER OF DREAMS AND A SEER OF VISIONS

George W. Norris was not a profound thinker. He added little in the way of intellectual innovation to American political thought. His political theory, particularly his agrarianism and his belief in the common man, included portions of the Jefferson-Jackson heritage. He adopted the moralistic conceptions of the Social Gospel and Christian Socialism; he accepted some of the propositions of Populism, and ultimately espoused Charles McCarthy's New Individualism. Yet this eclecticism in no way diminishes his importance to the American tradition of reform. For although the Nebraskan's thinking was a merger of swirling, and often contradictory, intellectual currents, he was able to bring them to a satisfactory confluence and to be a doer who made a lasting contribution to American democracy.

The Norris-LaGuardia Act, the Norris-Doxey Act, and the Norris-Rayburn Act were in keeping with the finest expressions of a combined agrarian-urban progressive spirit. The enactment of the Twentieth Amendment to the Constitution and the establishment of Nebraska's unicameral legislature, both due primarily to Norris' influence, were designed to make government more effective and more responsive to the desires of the electorate. But Norris' most lasting achievement was propagating the idea of the responsibility of the government to all its citizens. This conception of the ethical functions of the state saw its fruition in the establish-

[10] Arthur S. Link, "What Happened to the Progressive Movement in the 1920's?" *The Progressive Era: Liberal Renaissance or Liberal Failure?* ed. Arthur Mann (New York: Holt, Rinehart and Winston, 1963), pp. 115–16, 117. Professor Mann has gathered in this volume choice selections of the various interpretations of progressivism.

ment of the Tennessee Valley Authority. The Senator's contributions to the welfare state, particularly in the creation of the TVA,
cannot be minimized. He was willing to utilize the device of a
government corporation and all that it implied in its rejection of
laissez-faire. And he was willing to accept the principle of federal
regulation in order to protect society's weak and oppressed.

Perhaps the easiest way to understand George W. Norris, and
to excuse his shortcomings, both intellectual and personal, would
be to characterize him as an emotional liberal who had an abiding
and passionate devotion to the concerns of his fellow men. Basically, Norris was a moral idealist in politics. Although at times
Norris fought a losing battle in attempting to restore an age which
was past, particularly in his acceptance of the agrarian myth, paradoxically, his advocacy of the positive state kept him in the vanguard of the American reform tradition. He was a spokesman of
the past, but at the same time he held a vision of the future.

Despite his occasional flights into pessimism, Norris always predicated his actions on a struggle theory which was basically for-
ward-looking and evangelical. The mass of mankind, he believed,
was good, and therefore, the people would triumph despite the
barriers placed before them. The concluding paragraphs of his
Autobiography are a testament to his faith in America, his belief
in the gospel of democracy, and his moral approach to politics: "I
am sure that, from among America's fighting men and others, war-
riors will appear to fight the unending battle for good government.
I am sure that, so long as there are men, there will be knights to
lift their swords and press shields against the enemies, corruption
and evil. Liberalism will not die." [11]

Norris always fought the unending battle for good government.
He fought this battle in the years preceding the Armageddon of
1912 and in the years after it. Another progressive, Harold L. Ickes,
the self-styled "Old Curmudgeon" who was notoriously close-
mouthed in praise of his fellow human beings, bestowed on Norris
the rare accolade that he was "one of the best representatives that
the people ever had in the United States Senate." [12] Ickes was correct. George W. Norris' long congressional tenure, the ultimate

[11] George W. Norris, *Fighting Liberal: The Autobiography of George W. Norris* (New York: The Macmillan Company, 1945), p. 410.
[12] Harold L. Ickes, *The Secret Diary of Harold L. Ickes: The Lowering Clouds* (New York: Simon and Schuster, Inc., 1954), p. 652.

acceptance of many of the things for which he fought, and his embodiment of the characteristics of integrity, independence, and liberalism properly earned for him the status of a folk hero in the finest traditions of American political life.

Chronology

☆ ☆ ☆ ☆ ☆ ☆ ☆ ☆ ☆

GEORGE W. NORRIS (July 11, 1861–September 3, 1944)

1861 Born, York Township, Ohio

1877 Teaches country school, Monclova Township, Ohio

1880 Receives Bachelor of Science degree from Northern Indiana Normal School (now Valparaiso University), Indiana

1885 Opens a law office in Beaver City, Nebraska

1890 Makes first bid for political office. Loses to Populist candidate in race for office of prosecuting attorney of Furnas County, Nebraska

1892 Elected prosecutor of Furnas County, Nebraska

1895 Elected judge of 14th Nebraska District Court

1898 Re-elected judge, moves to McCook, Nebraska

1902 Elected to House of Representatives for 5th District, Nebraska; re-elected in 1904, 1906, 1908, 1910

1904 Delivers maiden speech, "On the Extension of Civil Service," in House

1908 First evidence of insurgency; introduces a resolution calling for all standing committees to be appointed by the Committee on Rules

1909   Successfully opposes Speaker Cannon on issue of members of Ballinger-Pinchot investigating committee

1910   Leads revolt against Speaker Cannon; wins passage of resolution that the House, not the Speaker, appoint members of the Rules Committee

1911   Elected a vice-president of the National Progressive Republican League

1912   Elected to Senate under the "Oregon System"

1917   Filibusters against passage of Armed Ship bill and is one of six senators to vote against Declaration of War on Germany

1918   Re-elected to second term in Senate

1920   Active in establishment of Peoples' Legislative Service

1922   Acts as chairman of Progressive Conference

1924   Re-elected to third term in Senate

1928   Refuses nomination for Presidency offered by Minnesota Farmer-Labor convention but permits his name to be used in Wisconsin and Nebraska presidential primaries. Endorses Democratic presidential candidate Alfred E. Smith

1930   Despite "Grocer Norris" campaign incident, is re-elected to fourth term in Senate

1931   Active in Conference of Progressives

1932   Passage of Norris-LaGuardia Federal Anti-Injunction Act; passage of 20th Amendment to the Constitution ending "lame duck" congressional sessions

1933   Passage of Tennessee Valley Authority Act

1936   Re-elected to fifth term in Senate as an Independent; passage of the Norris-Rayburn Rural Electrification Act

1937   Successfully leads fight for establishment of a unicameral legislature in Nebraska; passage of Norris-Doxey Farm Forestry Law

1942   Runs for sixth term in Senate but is defeated

1944   Dies, McCook, Nebraska

Bibliography

☆　☆　☆　☆　☆　☆　☆　☆　☆

PRIMARY SOURCES

Unpublished Material

George W. Norris Papers. Manuscripts Division, Library of Congress.

Norris, George W. "Criminal Procedure in Our Courts," June 24, 1928.

——. "The Eagle or the Parrot," n.d.

——. "The Federal Trade Commission," November 17, 1925.

——. "If I were President," n.d.

——. "Keeping the Railroads Out of Politics," n.d.

——. "Partisanship," October 17, 1932.

——. "Statement," n.d.

——. "Statement Concerning the Lame Duck," January 20, 1933.

——. "Statement: In re Norris Railroad Bill," n.d.

Published Material

books

La Follette, Robert M. *A Personal Narrative of Political Experiences.* Madison: University of Wisconsin Press, 1961.

McCarthy, Charles. *The Wisconsin Idea.* New York: The Macmillan Company, 1912.

Nixon, Edgar B., ed. *Franklin D. Roosevelt and Conservation: 1911–1945.* Washington, D.C.: Government Printing Office, 1957.

Norris, George W. *Fighting Liberal: The Autobiography of George W. Norris.* New York: The Macmillan Company, 1945.

————. *Peace Without Hate*. Lincoln: University of Nebraska Press, 1943.

Porter, Kirk H., and Johnson, Donald Bruce, compilers. *National Party Platforms, 1840–1960*. Urbana: University of Illinois Press, 1961.

Conference of Progressives, *Proceedings* (Washington, D.C., March 11 and 12, 1931).

PERIODICALS

Norris, George W. "Abolish Federal Courts?" *New York Times Magazine*, April 23, 1922, p. 5.

————. "Abolition of the Electoral College," *United States Law Review*, LXVIII (June 1934), 287–91.

————. "Boring from Within," *The Nation*, CXXI (September 16, 1925), 297–99.

————. "Bryan as a Political Leader," *Current History*, XXII (September 1925), 859–67.

————. "Coddling the Lame Duck," *The Independent*, CXIV (February 21, 1925), 213–14.

————. "The Farmers' Situation, a National Danger," *Current History*, XXIV (April 1926), 9–13.

————. "The Future of the Negro in Politics," *The Crisis*, XXXVIII (September 1931), 297–98.

————. "Germany After Defeat," *New Republic*, CX (May 22, 1944), 703–5.

————. "A Model State Legislature," *New York Times Magazine*, January 28, 1923, p. 12.

————. "My Party Right or Wrong," *Colliers*, LXXIII (June 21, 1924), 5–8.

————. "The One-House Legislature," *The Annals of the American Academy of Political and Social Science*, CLXXXVI (September 1935), 50–58.

————. "The One-House Legislature," *National Municipal Review*, XXIV (February 1935), 87–89.

————. "The Pennsylvania Patriot's Duty: Elect a Democrat," *The Nation*, CXXIII (July 14, 1926), 28–29.

————. "Politics and Your Electricity Bills," *Plain Talk* (July 1928). Reprinted in *Congressional Record*, Vol. 71, pt. 2, 1521 (May 30, 1929).

————. "Possibilities of the Completed Plant," *Current History*, XXVIII (August 1928), 730–33.

————. "Put Not Your Faith in Parties," *The Nation*, CXVIII (April 2, 1924), 369.

————. "Shall We Give Muscle Shoals to Henry Ford?" *The Saturday Evening Post*, CXCVI (May 31, 1924), 125–27.

————. "The Tariff and the Farmer," *The Nation*, CXXIII (September 1, 1926), 192–93.

————. "U.S. Must Save Britain Even if It Means War," *The Sunday Oregonian*, September 14, 1941, p. 1.

————. "What Democracy Means to Me," *Scholastic*, XXXII (May 28, 1932), 29.

————. "Why the Farm Bloc," *The World Tomorrow*, II (June 1928), 255–58.

————. "Why Henry Ford Wants Muscle Shoals," *The Nation*, CXVII (December 26, 1923), 738–40.

————. "Why I Am a Better Republican Than President Hoover," *Liberty*, September 24, 1932, pp. 13–16.

————. "Why I Believe in the Direct Primary," *The Annals of the American Academy of Political and Social Science*, CVI (March 1923), 22–30.

MISCELLANEOUS PUBLIC ADDRESSES

Norris, George W. "Address at Lincoln Monument Unveiling at Freeport, Illinois," August 27, 1929. Reprinted in *Congressional Record*, Vol. 71, pt. 3, 3421–25 (September 9, 1929).

————. "Address at the University of Illinois on Receiving the Cardinal Newman Award," November 16, 1933. Reprinted in *Congressional Record*, Vol. 78, pt. 1, 519–23 (January 12, 1934).

————. "American Neutrality," Radio Address, October 3, 1939. Reprinted in *Congressional Record*, Vol. 85, pt. 2, Appendix, 128–30 (October 4, 1939).

————. "Behind the Political Smokescreen," Radio Address over the Columbia Broadcasting System, June 14, 1936. Reprinted in *Congressional Record*, Vol. 80, pt. 9, 9604–7 (June 16, 1936).

————. "A Finer Life on Nebraska Farms," Address at Lincoln, Nebraska, January 4, 1937. Reprinted in *Congressional Record*, Vol. 81, pt. 9, 52–54 (January 19, 1937).

————. "The Lend-Lease Bill," Radio Address, February 26, 1941. Reprinted in *Congressional Record*, Vol. 87, pt. 10, A873–A875 (February 27, 1941).

————. "A Nonpartisan Party," Address before First National Conference of Popular Government, Washington, D.C., December 6, 1913. *Senate Document 372*, 63rd Congress, 2nd Session. Washington, D.C.: Government Printing Office, 1914.

————. "A Pagan Philosophy of Government," Commencement Address at Wooster College, Ohio, June 10, 1941. Reprinted in *Congressional Record*, Vol. 87, pt. 12, AA2862–AA2865 (June 16, 1941).

————. "Redistribution of Wealth," *Vital Speeches of the Day*, I (February 25, 1932), 329–33.

————. Remarks in the House of Representatives and the Senate of the United States, 1903–42. *Congressional Record*, 1903–42.

GOVERNMENT DOCUMENTS AND REPORTS

"George W. Norris: Proceedings in Connection with the Testimonial Dinner Given on December 10, 1942, Washington, D.C.," *Senate Document No. 292*, 77th Congress, 2nd Session. Washington, D.C.: Government Printing Office, 1942.

Norris, George W. "Agricultural Export Bill," *Senate Report No. 193*, 68th Congress, 1st Session. Washington, D.C.: Government Printing Office, March 5, 1924.

————. "Farmers' Export Finance Corporation Act," *Senate Report No. 192*, 67th Congress, 1st Session. Washington, D.C.: Government Printing Office, June 30, 1921.

————. "Fixing the Commencement of Terms of President, Vice-President, and Members of Congress," *Senate Report No. 170*, 68th Congress, 1st Session. Washington, D.C.: Government Printing Office, February 22, 1924.

————. "Limiting the Jurisdiction of District Courts of the United States," *Senate Report No. 626*, 70th Congress, 1st Session. Washington, D.C.: Government Printing Office, March 27, 1928.

————. "Merit System in the Post Office," *Senate Document No. 439*, 64th Congress, 1st Session. Washington, D.C.: Government Printing Office, 1916.

SECONDARY SOURCES

UNPUBLISHED MATERIAL

Beaven, Winton Henry. *A Critical Analysis and Appraisal of the Public Address of Senator George W. Norris.* Ph.D. thesis, University of Michigan, Ann Arbor: University Microfilms No. 1947, 1950.

Effross, Harris I. *The Political Philosophy of Herbert Croly.* Unpublished Ph.D. thesis, Rutgers University, 1959.

Ellis, Clyde T. "The Norris Mission: Key to the Western World," *Remarks Before the George W. Norris Centennial Conference.* Washington, D.C.: May 16, 1961.

Danker, Donald Floyd. *Senator George W. Norris and Federal Water Power Legislation.* Unpublished Master's thesis, University of Nebraska, 1949.

PUBLISHED MATERIAL

BOOKS

Adler, Selig. *The Isolationist Impulse: Its Twentieth-Century Reaction.* London and New York: Abelard-Schuman Ltd., 1957.

Alsop, Joseph, and Catledge, Turner. *The 168 Days.* New York: Doubleday, Doran and Company, Inc., 1938.

Bagby, Wesley M. *The Road to Normalcy: The Presidential Campaign and Election of 1920.* Baltimore: The Johns Hopkins Press, 1962.

Benedict, Murray R. *Farm Policies of the United States, 1790–1950: A Study of Their Origins and Development.* New York: The Twentieth Century Fund, 1953.

Bernstein, Irving. *The Lean Years: A History of the American Worker 1920–1933.* Boston: Houghton Mifflin Company, 1960.

Breckenridge, Adam C. *One House for Two: Nebraska's Unicameral Legislature.* Washington, D.C.: Public Affairs Press, 1957.

Burdette, Franklin L. *Filibustering in the Senate.* Princeton: Princeton University Press, 1940.

Burns, Edward McNall. *The American Idea of Mission: Concepts of National Purpose and Destiny.* New Brunswick: Rutgers University Press, 1957.

Cochran, Thomas C., and Miller, William. *The Age of Enterprise: A Social History of Industrial America* (rev. ed.). New York: Harper Torchbooks, 1961.

Cox, Archibald. *Law and the National Labor Policy.* Los Angeles: Institute of Industrial Relations, University of California, 1960.

Coyle, David Cushman. *Conservation.* New Brunswick: Rutgers University Press, 1957.

Dulles, Foster Rhea. *Labor in America.* New York: Thomas Y. Crowell Company, 1949.

Fainsod, Merle, Gordon, Lincoln, and Palamountain, Joseph C., Jr. *Government and the American Economy.* New York: W. W. Norton and Company, Inc., 1959.

Fine, Sidney. *Laissez Faire and the General Welfare State: A Study of Conflict in American Thought, 1865–1901.* Ann Arbor: University of Michigan Press, 1956.

Firth, Robert E. *Public Power in Nebraska: A Report on State Ownership.* Lincoln: University of Nebraska Press, 1962.

Glad, Paul W. *The Trumpet Soundeth: William Jennings Bryan and His Democracy, 1896–1912.* Lincoln: University of Nebraska Press, 1960.

Goldman, Eric F. *Rendezvous with Destiny: A History of Modern American Reform.* New York: Vintage Books, 1956.

Gregory, Charles O. *Labor and the Law.* New York: W. W. Norton and Company, Inc., 1946.

Hays, Samuel P. *Conservation and the Gospel of Efficiency: The Progressive Conservation Movement, 1890–1920.* Cambridge: Harvard University Press, 1959.

Hechler, Kenneth W. *Insurgency: Personalities and Politics of the Taft Era.* New York: Columbia University Press, 1940.

Hicks, John D. *The Populist Revolt: A History of the Farmers' Alliance and the People's Party*. Minneapolis: University of Minnesota Press, 1931.

―――. *Rehearsal for Disaster: The Boom and Collapse of 1919–1920*. Gainesville: University of Florida Press, 1961.

Higham, John, ed. *The Reconstruction of American History*. New York: Harper and Brothers, 1962.

Hofstadter, Richard. *The Age of Reform: From Bryan to F.D.R.* New York: Alfred A. Knopf, 1956.

―――. *The American Political Tradition*. New York: Vintage Books, 1954.

―――. *Social Darwinism in American Thought* (rev. ed.). Boston: Beacon Press, 1955.

Hubbard, Preston J. *Origins of the TVA: The Muscle Shoals Controversy, 1920–1932*. Nashville: Vanderbilt University Press, 1961.

Ickes, Harold L. *The Secret Diary of Harold L. Ickes: The Lowering Clouds*. New York: Simon and Schuster, Inc., 1954.

Johnson, Alvin W. *The Unicameral Legislature*. Minneapolis: University of Minnesota Press, 1938.

Johnson, Claudius O. "George William Norris," *The American Politician*, ed. J. T. Salter. Chapel Hill: University of North Carolina Press, 1938, pp. 77–108.

Key, V. O., Jr. *Politics, Parties, and Pressure Groups*. New York: Thomas Y. Crowell Company, 1958.

King, Judson. *The Conservation Fight: From Theodore Roosevelt to the Tennessee Valley Authority*. Washington, D.C.: Public Affairs Press, 1959.

Leuchtenburg, William E. *Franklin D. Roosevelt and the New Deal, 1932–1940*. New York: Harper and Row, 1963.

―――. *The Perils of Prosperity: 1914–1932*. Chicago: University of Chicago Press, 1958.

Lief, Alfred. *Democracy's Norris: The Biography of a Lonely Crusade*. New York: Stackpole Sons, 1939.

Lilienthal, David E. *TVA: Democracy on the March*. New York: Harper and Brothers, 1944.

Link, Arthur S. *American Epoch: A History of the United States Since the 1890's*. New York: Alfred A. Knopf, 1956.

―――. *Woodrow Wilson and the Progressive Era: 1910–1917*. New York: Harper and Brothers, 1954.

Lowitt, Richard. *George W. Norris: The Making of a Progressive, 1861–1912*. Syracuse: Syracuse University Press, 1963.

McCoy, Donald R. *Angry Voices: Left-of-Center Politics in the New Deal Era*. Lawrence: University of Kansas Press, 1958.

McCune, Wesley. *The Farm Bloc*. New York: Doubleday, Doran and Company, Inc., 1943.

MacKay, Kenneth Campbell. *The Progressive Movement of 1924*. New York: Columbia University Press, 1947.

Madison, Charles A. *Leaders and Liberals in Twentieth Century America*. New York: Frederick Ungar Publishing Co., Inc., 1961.

Mann, Arthur. *LaGuardia: A Fighter Against His Times, 1882–1933*. Philadelphia: J. B. Lippincott Co., 1959.

————, ed. *The Progressive Era: Liberal Renaissance or Liberal Failure?* New York: Holt, Rinehart and Winston, 1963.

Mason, Alpheus Thomas. *Bureaucracy Convicts Itself: The Ballinger-Pinchot Controversy of 1910*. New York: The Viking Press, 1941.

Metz, Harold W. *Labor Policy and the Federal Government*. Washington, D.C.: The Brookings Institution, 1945.

Mowry, George E. *The Era of Theodore Roosevelt: 1900–1912*. New York: Harper and Brothers, 1958.

————. *The Progressive Movement, 1900–1920: Recent Ideas and New Literature*. Washington, D.C.: American Historical Assoc., 1958.

Nash, Howard P., Jr. *Third Parties in American Politics*. Washington, D.C.: Public Affairs Press, 1959.

Nelson, Ralph L. *Merger Movements in American Industry, 1895–1956*. Princeton: Princeton University Press, 1959.

Neuberger, Richard L., and Kahn, Stephen B. *Integrity: The Life of George W. Norris*. New York: Vanguard Press, 1937.

Nye, Russel B. *Midwestern Progressive Politics: A Historical Study of Its Origins and Development, 1870–1958*. East Lansing: Michigan State University Press, 1959.

Peterson, H. C., and Fite, Gilbert C. *Opponents of War 1917–1918*. Madison: University of Wisconsin Press, 1957.

Pritchett, C. Herman. *The American Constitution*. New York: McGraw-Hill Book Co., Inc., 1959.

————. *The Tennessee Valley Authority: A Study in Public Administration*. Chapel Hill: University of North Carolina Press, 1943.

Prothro, James Warren. *The Dollar Decade: Business Ideas in the 1920's*. Baton Rouge: Louisiana State University Press, 1954.

Ranney, Austin. *The Doctrine of Responsible Party Government*. Urbana: University of Illinois Press, 1954.

Saloutos, Theodore, and Hicks, John D. *Agricultural Discontent in the Middle West, 1900–1939*. Madison: University of Wisconsin Press, 1951.

Schattschneider, E. E. *Party Government*. New York: Rinehart and Company, Inc., 1942.

Seidman, Joel I. *The Yellow-Dog Contract*. Baltimore: The Johns Hopkins Press, 1932.

Senning, John P. *The One-House Legislature*. New York: McGraw-Hill Book Co., Inc., 1937.

Shideler, James H. *Farm Crisis: 1919–1923.* Berkeley and Los Angeles: University of California Press, 1957.

Timberlake, James H. *Prohibition and the Progressive Movement: 1900–1920.* Cambridge: Harvard University Press, 1963.

Toward a More Responsible Two-Party System. Report of the Committee on Political Parties of the American Political Science Association. New York: Rinehart and Company, Inc., 1950.

Tucker, Ray, and Barkley, Frederick R. *Sons of the Wild Jackass.* Boston: L. C. Page and Company, 1932.

Weinberg, Arthur and Lila, eds. *The Muckrakers, the Era in Journalism That Moved America to Reform — Significant Magazine Articles of 1902–1912.* New York: Simon and Schuster, Inc., 1961.

White, Morton. *Social Thought in America: The Revolt Against Formalism.* Boston: Beacon Press, 1957.

Whitney, Simon N. *Antitrust Policies: American Experience in the Twenty Industries.* New York: The Twentieth Century Fund, 1958.

Wilmerding, Lucius, Jr. *The Electoral College.* New Brunswick: Rutgers University Press, 1958.

Wilson, H. H. *Congress, Corruption, and Compromise.* New York: Rinehart and Company, Inc., 1951.

PERIODICALS

Beck, James M. "Can a Senator-Elect Be Denied His Seat?" *Congressional Digest,* VI (November 1927), 305–8.

Fellman, David. "The Liberalism of Senator Norris," *American Political Science Review,* XL (February 1946), 27–51.

Fite, Gilbert C. "Equality for the Farmer," *Current History,* XXVI (February 1954), 91–98.

Geiser, Karl F. "Defects in the Direct Primary," *The Annals of the American Academy of Political and Social Science,* CVI (March 1923), 31–39.

Hinton, Harold. "This Is Not Like 1917 — Says Norris," *New York Times Magazine,* July 6, 1941, p. 7.

Janson, Donald. "The House Nebraska Built," *Harper's Magazine,* CCXXIX (November 1964), 124–30.

Leuchtenburg, William E. "Roosevelt, Norris and the 'Seven Little TVA's,'" *Journal of Politics,* XIV (August 1952), 418–41.

Locke, Walter. "George W. Norris, Independent," *Antioch Review,* V (June 1945), 274–84.

Lowitt, Richard. "Norris and Nebraska, 1885–1890," *Nebraska History,* XXXIX (March 1958), 23–39.

———. "The Ohio Boyhood of George W. Norris," *Northwest Ohio Quarterly,* XXX (Spring 1958), 70–77.

———. "Populism and Politics: The Start of George W. Norris' Political Career," *Nebraska History,* XLII (June 1961), 75–94.

Lowitt, Richard, and Downes, Randolph C., eds. "George W. Norris: Monclova Township Schoolmaster," *Northwest Ohio Quarterly*, XXX (Spring 1958), 78–91.

Neuberger, Richard L. "A Politician Unafraid: George W. Norris, Senator from Nebraska," *Harper's Magazine*, CLXXIII (September 1936), 540–50.

Obituary of Senator George W. Norris. *Commonweal*, XL (September 15, 1944), 508.

Robbins, L. H. "Norris Restates a Liberal's Credo," *New York Times Magazine*, May 30, 1937, p. 3.

Shumate, Roger V. "The Nebraska Unicameral Legislature," *Western Political Quarterly*, V (September 1952), 504–12.

Tucker, Ray. "Norris Surveys the Political Scene," *New York Times Magazine*, July 14, 1935, p. 3.

Villard, Oswald Garrison. "Pillars of Government: George W. Norris," *Forum*, XCV (April 1936), 249–53.

Wilcox, Ralph F. "Intensive Forestry Projects Under the Provisions of the Cooperative Farm Forestry Act," *Journal of Forestry*, XXXVIII (June 1940), 457–64.

Index

☆   ☆   ☆   ☆   ☆   ☆   ☆   ☆   ☆

33555

DATE DUE

GAYLORD			PRINTED IN U.S.A.